GOVERNORS STATE UNIVERSITY LIBRARY

3 1611 00351 2990

Becoming an
EMOTIONALLY
INTELLIGENT
TEACHER

W9-CHP-355

GOVERNORS STATE UNIVERSITY
UNIVERSITY PARK
IL 60466

Becoming an
EMOTIONALLY
INTELLIGENT
TEACHER

GOVERNORS STATE UNIVERSITY
UNIVERSITY PARK
IL 60466

William Powell
Ochan Kusuma-Powell

Foreword by
Arthur L. Costa and Robert J. Garmston

CORWIN
A SAGE Company

LB
1072
.P69
2010

Copyright © 2010 by Corwin

All rights reserved. When forms and sample documents are included, their use is authorized only by educators, local school sites, and/or noncommercial or nonprofit entities that have purchased the book. Except for that usage, no part of this book may be reproduced or utilized in any form or by any means, electronic or mechanical, including photocopying, recording, or by any information storage and retrieval system, without permission in writing from the publisher.

For information:

Corwin
A SAGE Company
2455 Teller Road
Thousand Oaks, California 91320
(800) 233-9936
Fax: (800) 417-2466
www.corwin.com

SAGE India Pvt. Ltd.
B 1/I 1 Mohan Cooperative
    Industrial Area
Mathura Road, New Delhi 110 044
India

SAGE Ltd.
1 Oliver's Yard
55 City Road
London EC1Y 1SP
United Kingdom

SAGE Asia-Pacific Pte. Ltd.
33 Pekin Street #02-01
Far East Square
Singapore 048763

Printed in the United States of America

Library of Congress Cataloging-in-Publication Data

Powell, William R.
Becoming an emotionally intelligent teacher / William R. Powell, Ochan Kusuma-Powell; foreword by Arthur L. Costa and Robert J. Garmston.
        p. cm.
Includes bibliographical references and index.
ISBN 978-1-4129-7974-0 (pbk.)
    1. Affective education. 2. Emotional intelligence. 3. Emotions and cognition.
I. Kusuma-Powell, Ochan. II. Title.

LB1072.P69 2010
370.15'34—dc22   2009035964

This book is printed on acid-free paper.

10   11   12   13   14   10   9   8   7   6   5   4   3   2   1

Acquisitions Editor:	Hudson Perigo
Associate Editors:	Julie McNall and Joanna Coelho
Editorial Assistant:	Allison Scott
Production Editor:	Amy Schroller
Copy Editor:	Cynthia Long
Typesetter:	C&M Digitals (P) Ltd.
Proofreader:	Ellen Howard
Indexer:	Judy Hunt
Cover Designer:	Karine Hovsepian

Contents

Foreword

Imagine yourself in a comfortable and casual setting. You listen in to a conversation and realize you are mesmerized by the talk. These authors clearly know the world you occupy, and you are captivated by the clarity, insight, and knowledge they display. But wait. Something is amiss. These men and women come from separate disciplines, some you normally wouldn't attempt to read, much less try to understand. But here they are, speaking matter-of-factly and down-to-earth with Bill and Ochan Powell providing glue and applications to their work with authentic, compelling, and sometimes humorous stories about school.

Drawing on vast research and years of personal experience, the Powells convey through vibrant school examples, appealing human vignettes, and illustrative classroom narratives that how teachers respond to stress, what teachers profess as their beliefs, how teachers adapt to classroom diversity, and how teachers process learning in their own style has a profound effect on student learning. The authors' vivid, personal, and intimate writing style brings us into classrooms, staff meetings, and parent conferences, and like a welcome but invisible observer, we interact with the personalities of numerous teachers, students, parents, and administrators as they deal with the complexities of school life. Magically, breaking through the usual fragmentation and academic language, the Powells create a practical book for every teacher and every person who works with teachers. Listen with them as they blend teaching implications with research from such fields as education, social psychology, anthropology, sociology, and neuroscience.

Meet Carmen, Matthias, Irshad, Melvin, Grace, Marina, Nishad, Pauline, and Stefano and other multinational students in stories of authentic challenges and celebrations teachers face. You'll get to know and feel like you're sitting beside Malcom Rigby during a grade-level meeting, observing in the classroom of Miss Elizabeth Crawley, or entering the case study of a student named Jonathan. These personalized, charming vignettes make the text come alive to help you understand the realities of school dynamics.

The authors of this book are not only educators, long practiced in our profession, but are accomplished authors. They write with compassion and have the ability to enter the world of students, teachers, and support personnel. They understand their insecurities, passions, and worries. They practice emotional, contextual, and cognitive empathy providing not simple answers but authentic responses to complex interactions. Each page has a sense of immediacy; the prose is tight and quick. The headings, such as "Pygmalion on Her First Date," "Let Them Learn Chinese!" "The Marshmallow Challenge," "Margaret: The Loose Cannon," "If Teaching Involves Acting, What Does the Audience Think?" and others, invite curiosity and draw us into the fascinating world of the schoolhouse.

For teachers, this book provides validation for the school and classroom situations in which they find themselves. As teachers learn more about themselves and understand personal stressors, this book provides practical suggestions for ways to respond. This tidy compendium of wisdom brings special gifts. First, the book validates all shades of teaching experiences without judgment. Next, it provides research-based answers to why teachers react and feel as they do in challenging situations. It offers not only practical tips borne of the authors' experience but activities that enhance their capacities for emotionally intelligent teaching. Finally, this extraordinary book enhances teachers' capacity for self-management, self-monitoring, and self-modification toward their own gain and the learning of students.

What do students learn that is not explicitly taught? While curriculum committees labor to map the curriculum, compose essential questions, decide on what's most worth knowing, clarify academic outcomes, and formulate assessment rubrics, we must also remember that children's most enduring learning may not be found in standards, benchmarks, and exit exams. Their most essential and lifelong learning stems from the display of their teacher's level of emotional maturity in the moment-to-moment response to the twists and turns of daily classroom life.

Students learn best through imitation of significant others. Research with mirror neurons suggests that imitation and emulation are the most basic forms of learning. Teachers, parents, and administrators realize the importance of their own modeling of desirable habits in the presence of learners. In the day-to-day events and when problems arise in schools, classrooms, and homes, children must see the significant adults employing positive, rational, thoughtful, trusting behaviors. Without this consistency, there will be a credibility gap that, in turn, produces stress that distracts from and even negates deep learning. As Ralph Waldo Emerson is quoted as saying, "What you do speaks so loudly that I cannot hear what you say."

Since most student learning is "caught, not taught," the purpose of this book is to enhance teacher congruity in working with students. It encourages authentic and rational responses to situations, which in turn, allows students to respond with authenticity to the complex situations that they will encounter throughout their lifetimes.

—Arthur L. Costa, EdD, and Robert J. Garmston, EdD
Professors Emeriti, California State University
Sacramento, California

Preface

How to Use This Book

This book is written for classroom teachers, aspiring educators, school administrators, staff developers, and others with an interest in the relationships between teacher emotional intelligence and student learning.

It is based on two premises. The first is that teachers who have strong emotional intelligence support more effective and efficient student learning than those with only limited emotional intelligence. We will offer considerable evidence to support this contention. The second premise is that although some people seem to be born with excellent interpersonal skills and others not, emotional intelligence is malleable and can be developed. Put simply, teachers, even gifted ones, can choose to raise their emotional intelligence.

The structure of the book follows Daniel Goleman's (1995) five components of emotional intelligence (EQ) and represents an exploration of how these qualities relate to the work of classroom teachers, specialists, and administrators. The chapters focus on aspects of emotional self-awareness, self-regulation, motivation, social awareness, and relationship management.

Each chapter contains a discussion of some of the theoretical aspects of EQ illustrated with actual case studies drawn from the authors' more than 30 years experience in schools around the world. Following the theoretical discussion, each chapter includes a series of practical activities and exercises that teachers can use or staff developers can employ to facilitate professional development in the area of emotional intelligence.

The final chapter is a synthesis of the overarching ideas that connect teacher emotional intelligence with effective and efficient student learning.

Acknowledgments

The research for this book was funded by a grant from the East Asian Council of Overseas Schools (EARCOS), and we would like to express our appreciation to Dr. Dick Krajczar, the EARCOS executive director, for his support and encouragement. We would also like to express our appreciation to the Office of Overseas Schools at the U.S. State Department for ongoing support of our work in teacher professional development. Specifically, we would like to thank Dr. Keith Miller and Dr. Connie Buford. An abbreviated version of this book, titled *The Emotionally Intelligent International School Teacher: Why Teacher EQ Matters,* was published by EARCOS and was distributed to member schools.

There were many individuals who contributed to this book— knowingly and unknowingly. We would like to extend our gratitude to Bambi Betts, director of the Principals' Training Center and CEO of the Academy for International School Heads; Sue Williams, curriculum coordinator at the American School of the Hague; Kevin Bartlett, headmaster of the International School of Brussels; Walter Plotkin, superintendent of the American International School of Dhaka; Nick and Rhona Bowley (Council of International Schools and the American School of Milan respectively); Areta Williams, head of the Overseas School of Colombo; John Roberts, superintendent of the International School of Kenya; and Dennis MacKinnon, superintendent of the International School of Yangon.

From the International School of Kuala Lumpur, we would like to thank Naomi Aleman, the curriculum coordinator; Grant Millard, the high school principal; and Ochan's previous teaching partner, Alex Smith.

Finally, we would like to thank our old friends and mentors, Bob Garmston and Art Costa. Your support and encouragement has been greatly valued.

Corwin gratefully acknowledges the contributions of the peer reviewers who reviewed this book.

About the Authors

**William Powell** has served as a school educator for the past thirty years in the United States, Saudi Arabia, Tanzania, Indonesia, and Malaysia. From 1991 to 1999, he served as the chief executive officer of the International School of Tanganyika in Dar es Salaam, Tanzania; and from 2000 through 2006 as headmaster of the International School of Kuala Lumpur. He is the coauthor, with his wife Ochan, of *Count Me In! Developing Inclusive International Schools* (2000), and *Making the Difference: Differentiation in International Schools* (2007). Bill is a frequent contributor to educational journals and presents regularly at international educational conferences. Bill and Ochan have presented professional development workshops in more than forty different countries on five different continents. They focus their attention on teacher professional development and school leadership (Bpowell@eduxfrontiers.org). When he is not speaking at conferences, Bill can be found at his small farm in the French Pyrenees where he and a handful of sheep mount an annual battle against the European bramble.

Ochan Kusuma-Powell is cofounder and director of Education Across Frontiers, an organization that promotes teacher education toward the development of professional learning communities. A graduate of Columbia University with a doctorate in international education development, she has more than thirty years experience in international education. Ochan has developed and implemented inclusive special education programs in the United States, Indonesia, Malaysia, and Tanzania. She has been an outspoken advocate for children with special needs globally. Together with her husband, Bill, she coauthored an OSAC (Overseas Schools Advisory Council) publication titled *Count Me In! Developing Inclusive International Schools* (2000) and *Making the Difference: Differentiation in International Schools* (2007). Ochan is also the author of *Parent Advocacy in International Schools* (2008). She is a trainer for the Teachers Training Center and an adjunct faculty member at Lehigh University and the State University of New York at Buffalo. When she is not at 36,000 feet, Ochan can also be found in the French Pyrenees engaging her twin passions of reading and cooking.

List of Figures

Introduction

Not ignorance, but ignorance of ignorance is the death of knowledge.

—Alfred North Whitehead (n.d., para. 5)

Thomas wasn't having a good year in second grade. Handsome, athletic, and very socially sensitive, Thomas had a mild learning disability that was interfering with learning to read. He was also struggling with writing and basic arithmetic. He regularly failed to complete his work, and his teacher would have him stay in the classroom during recess to complete it. By mid-October, his classmates had picked up on the teacher's frustration with Thomas and were teasing him—calling him the "retard."

By November, Thomas was feigning illness to avoid going to school, and his mother was near despair. She had met with the teacher and the principal, and while they had developed a plan to get Thomas some extra tutoring in reading, this had done nothing to elevate Thomas's deep unhappiness and anxiety.

It was at this point that Thomas's mother brought her son for a consultation with Ochan, who was the coordinator of Special Services in the school. Initially, Thomas presented as a withdrawn and fearful child. He tended to avoid eye contact and would respond to Ochan's questions but would not initiate conversation. However, as the interview proceeded, Thomas became more comfortable and confident. He explained that he hated school because his teacher didn't like him. Ochan asked what made him believe this. Although socially astute and articulate, Thomas struggled with the question. He couldn't identify any specific comments or incidents, but he felt very strongly that the teacher's attitude toward him was one of disapproval and scorn.

We cannot know whether Thomas's perception of his teacher's attitude was accurate or not. We have no way of knowing what her true feelings about Thomas were. However, we can be certain that Thomas believed his perception to be accurate, and it was having a profoundly negative impact on his learning. His emotions were interfering with his learning.

We can also probably make the conjecture that the teacher was unaware of Thomas's perception or her own behavior that may have caused it. Very few teachers deliberately display their dislike for students. However, a teacher with limited EQ may do so without either intending to do so or even being aware of it.

Following the consultation, Ochan reviewed at length Thomas's previous school reports, his IEP (individual education plan) and his psycho-educational evaluation. While he did have a mild learning disability, it was not such that it should be causing the catastrophic emotional meltdown that Thomas was experiencing. It was, Ochan concluded, Thomas's perception that the teacher didn't like him that was the most significant obstacle to his learning.

Ochan discussed the matter with the principal and requested that Thomas be transferred to another class. After some discussion, the principal agreed. The new teacher had a far more positive attitude toward Thomas's learning challenges, and slowly he began again to learn to read. Today, Thomas is in his late twenties, reads voraciously but slowly, and teaches fourth grade.

Much has been written about how teachers can support the development of emotional intelligence in their students. Less has been written about the relationship between a teacher's own emotional intelligence and student learning.

Historically, educators have tended to dismiss or ignore the role of emotions in learning. From Descartes through the Age of Enlightenment, learning was seen as the province of the rational intellect, and our emotions were perceived to cloud or befuddle cognition.

There were, of course, a few who challenged this duality. In his eighteenth-century treatise on education, *Emile,* Jean-Jacques Rousseau (1762/1993) proposed that learning was a naturally occurring phenomenon that involves both our head and our heart. The Romantic poets celebrated the life of the emotions, and by the mid-nineteenth century, Charles Dickens (1854/2007) was writing scathingly in *Hard Times* about how education had been reduced to a "Gradgrindian" accumulation of facts.

Despite this handful of critics, there has been a widely held misconception that a duality exists between the intellect and the emotions; that cognition and the emotions are somehow separate and, in some cases, even diametrically opposed. This false dichotomy led to the belief that the brain was the seat of reason, logic, and analysis; whereas the emotions were irrational, counter to clear thinking, unpredictable, and generally suspect (especially in complex decision making). The traditional classroom has welcomed the intellect but has tacitly instructed children to leave their emotions with their hats and coats in their lockers. The assumption was that school learning was intellectual and that our emotions either played no role in such learning or might even serve as a hindrance to learning.

This was a serious misunderstanding of how emotions and cognition are inseparably connected. Research conducted over the last two decades demonstrates clearly that our emotional and intellectual lives do not run on separate tracks but are connected at a most basic level (Damasio, 1994; LeDoux, 1996; Pert, 1997).

We know now that all emotionally charged events receive preferential processing in the brain. They literally come to the front of the queue for processing, in some cases actually bypassing the neocortex. There are very good evolutionary reasons for this. For our cave-dwelling ancestors, emotionally charged events, for example, the charge of a woolly mammoth, evoked responses that were likely to be connected to survival and, more often than not, had significant future use.

Emotionally charged events also get preferential treatment in terms of our memory systems. Psychologists refer to this phenomenon as "flashbulb memory" (Brown & Kulik, 1977). Think back to when you first learned of an event connected to a powerful emotion: the assassination of John F. Kennedy or Martin Luther King Jr.; the *Challenger* tragedy; or more recently, the attacks of September 11, 2001. The chances are that you will be able to remember exactly where you were, what you were doing, and who you were with. Our emotions play a powerful role in determining what we pay attention to and what we select to remember. "An emotionally charged event is the best-processed kind of external stimulus ever measured. Emotionally charged events persist much longer in our memories and are recalled with greater accuracy than neutral memories" (Medina, 2008, p. 211).

There is compelling evidence that emotions also have a great deal to do with how we organize and create our sense of reality. Emotions drive how we prioritize our attention—what we select to focus upon and what we choose to ignore. They regulate our behavior and support us as we create meaning from the world around us.

Both in the classroom and outside it, emotions are sources of information about the physical and social world around us. Emotions associate our learning with pleasure or pain, as was the case with Thomas, and can result in retreat or perseverance. Emotions—the visceral thrill of a new insight or the excitement of a fresh mental connection—have the power to foster an enthusiasm for learning. This so-called hot cognition (Caine & Caine, 1994) is addictive and can lead to a passion for lifelong learning.

While teachers do not have absolute control over the emotional weather of the classroom, they have a powerful influence over the affective climate. More often than not, their verbal and nonverbal behaviors and their displays of emotion, dispositions, and moods can have powerful effects upon their students. The emotions that teachers display—both consciously and unconsciously—can significantly enhance or inhibit student learning.

A PROBLEM SO SIMPLE THAT EVEN BILL COULD SOLVE IT

As a child, Bill grew up in Britain. When he was eight, his teacher instructed him to go to the blackboard and solve a long-division problem involving the British currency then in circulation (pounds, shillings, and pence). This was a fairly complex procedure since Britain had not yet moved to the decimal system. There were four farthings in a penny, twelve pennies in a shilling, and twenty shillings in a pound. In front of the class, Bill struggled unsuccessfully with the problem. After a few minutes, the frustrated teacher came to the front of the classroom and announced that she would put on the board an arithmetic problem that was so simple that even Bill could solve it. She wrote up a three-digit addition problem. However, by this point Bill was feeling such intense stress that concentration was impossible. To the amusement of the rest of the class, Bill was unable to perform even the most basic calculations.

Clearly, the teacher exhibited a lack of one of the fundamental characteristics of EQ: empathy. And as a result, Bill's feelings of anxiety and humiliation interfered with his learning.

Recent brain research tells us a great deal about the effect of stress on learning. If high stress or powerful negative emotions have evoked the fight, flight, or freeze response, the amygdala (our emotional mission control) will block the passage of data into memory and will reduce the blood flow to the neocortex (the center of executive function and critical thinking) causing it to shut down (Sylwester, 2007).

WE TEND TO WORK HARDER FOR THOSE WHO CARE ABOUT US

Contrast the following scenario: During her elementary school years, Ochan's family moved a great deal (her father was employed by the United Nations). Her experience in school in Bangkok and New York had not been particularly successful, and Ochan had attributed her less-than-stellar performance to her own intellectual ability. That was until her dad was transferred to Addis Abba and Mrs. Joseph came into the picture.

Mrs. Joseph was a fourth-grade teacher at the Nazareth School in Addis. At the very start of the school year, she set out to come to know her students and to make personal connections to them. She expressed interest in her students and tried to design learning activities that would appeal to their learning styles. She was patient and cheerful. She cared deeply about her students and was unabashedly hopeful and optimistic about their achievement and progress. By the middle of the first term, Ochan reported to her parents that not only did she like Mrs. Joseph, but also she thought Mrs. Joseph liked her. For the first time, Ochan was enjoying school, and this was reflected in her increased effort. By the end of the year, Ochan's confidence, commitment, and competence had improved to such a degree that she was double promoted to the sixth grade.

In the United States, a nationwide survey of several hundred middle and high school students asked whether they worked harder for some teachers than for others. Three out of four of the teenagers answered in the affirmative, and the reason they gave was that these teachers cared about them. The authors of the survey concluded that effective schooling relies almost entirely on creative and passionate teachers (Crabtree, 2004).

TWO PREMISES

This book is based on two premises. The first is that teachers who have strong emotional intelligence (EQ), or social competence as it is sometimes called, create classroom environments that support more effective and efficient student learning than those teachers with only limited EQ. We will offer considerable evidence to support this contention. The second premise is that teachers can develop their emotional intelligence. Although some people seem to be born with excellent interpersonal skills and others not, emotional intelligence is malleable and can be learned. We believe that this is an area of teacher professional development that has been overlooked in the past and has rich potential for improving student learning.

The phrase *emotional intelligence* comes to us from the groundbreaking work of Reuven Bar-On (Bar-On & Parker, 2000) in the 1980s and the subsequent conceptualization of EQ by John Mayer and Peter Salovey (1997). It was popularized by a book with the same title by Daniel Goleman (1995). Goleman's contention is that emotional intelligence is actually more important in terms of success in life than what we have traditionally thought of as IQ. Subsequent to the publication of *Emotional*

Intelligence, Goleman has gone on to conduct significant research on emotional intelligence and its influence on leadership.

The study of emotional intelligence is a fairly radical departure from earlier behaviorist models of human interaction. Emotional intelligence looks beyond behavior. It assumes that behavior is purposeful, goal directed, and the product of cognition. Even negative and destructive behaviors are the product of thought and purposefulness.

Goleman (1995) identifies five components or domains of emotional intelligence: self-awareness, self-regulation, motivation, social awareness, and relationship management. While each of these domains is an essential part of the everyday life in classrooms around the world, most teacher training colleges treat them only on the periphery of the curriculum. One of the purposes of this book is to bring them center stage.

Emotions permeate classrooms while instruction is taking place. These are both the emotions of the students and the teacher. Whether these emotions are enthusiasm, excitement, boredom, frustration, anxiety, or anger— they are most certainly present. Recent research of the brain shows us that "neuronal pathways are activated through relational, emotional, personally relevant . . . and experiential stimuli. The repeated activation of these new circuits . . . will strengthen the new pathways . . . and increase the efficiency of memory retrieval" (Willis, 2007, pp. 19–20). In other words, emotions play a key role in learning—so key that we simply cannot afford to ignore them.

From experience, we know that teachers are called upon daily to manage and, at times, mask their emotions. When handled skillfully, such management can be seen as emotional competence. We would suggest that a high degree of teacher emotional competence is a prerequisite in any high-quality classroom.

Emotional competence allows us greater accuracy when we attempt to make sense of student behavior. Teaching is an interpretative activity. Hundreds of times each day, teachers are called upon to interpret student behavior. What did Julie's crinkled brow mean? Was Brian's tone of voice defiant? Did Rehema's nodding suggest understanding? Hundreds of times daily, we attempt to make sense of the emotions and feelings of our students. As such, teaching can be full of erroneous interpretations. Peer group pressure and intimidation can be invisible to teachers (Cushman, 2003). At times, we can mistake our own feelings for those of our students. At other times, we can mistake boredom for studious commitment or enthusiasm for hyperactivity. Confusion can become mistakenly construed as laziness as easily as attentiveness can be equated or misequated with comprehension. Accuracy of emotional interpretation is one of the most fundamental attributes of the effective teacher. When emotional understanding is absent, emotional misunderstanding will take its place.

Almost forty years ago, Haim Ginott (1995) addressed the question of whether teacher emotions influence their work performance and have an impact on student learning:

> I've come to a frightening conclusion that I am the decisive element in the classroom. It's my personal approach that creates the climate. It's my daily mood that makes the weather. As a teacher, I possess a tremendous power to make a child's life miserable or joyous. I can be a tool of torture or an instrument of inspiration. I can humiliate or humor, hurt or heal. In all situations, it is my response that decides whether a crisis will be escalated or de-escalated, and a child humanized or dehumanized. (pp. 15–16)

For these reasons we would contend that the emotional intelligence of teachers is as important to student learning as their subject-area mastery or the breadth of their repertoire of instructional strategies. The good news is that we can all develop enhanced skills in emotional intelligence.

1 Emotional Intelligence

*What It Is and
Why It Is So Important
in the Classroom*

Hence I have come to feel that the outcomes of teaching are either unimportant or hurtful. When I look back at the results of my past teaching, the real results seem the same—either damage was done or nothing significant occurred. . . . As a consequence, I realize that I am only interested in being a learner, preferably learning things that matter, that have some significant influence on my own behavior. . . . I find that one of the best, but most difficult ways for me to learn is to drop my own defensiveness, at least temporarily, and try to understand the way in which his experience seems and feels to the other person. I find that another way of learning is for me to state my own uncertainties, to try to clarify my puzzlements and thus get closer to the meaning that my experience actually seems to have. . . . It seems to mean letting my experience carry me on, in a direction which appears to be forward, toward goals that I can but dimly define, as I try to understand at least the current meaning of that experience.

—Carl Rogers (1961, pp. 276–277)

I am always ready to learn although I do not always like being taught.

—Winston Churchill (1952, para. 1)

AN EMOTIONALLY INTELLIGENT CONVERSATION

In different ways, the quotations from Carl Rogers and Winston Churchill focus on one of the most ancient and profound misunderstandings in education: the assumption that there is always a direct and causal relationship between teaching and learning. Both authors suggest that in their respective experiences, there were times when *teaching* did not produce the *facilitation of learning.* To the contrary, Rogers suggests (and Churchill implies) that teaching can be hurtful and even destructive to learning. If this is the case, we are compelled to ask, "What are the conditions under which teaching does produce the facilitation of learning?"

When Stephen was ready to move from the eighth to ninth grade, his mother was filled with trepidation. Although Stephen wasn't a strong academic student, he had had a moderately successful year in the eighth grade. He had had caring, sensitive teachers who worked to support Stephen both academically and in terms of his self-confidence. Stephen was now on the cusp of entering a college-preparatory high school program, and his mother was deeply concerned that the emphasis on academic rigor would be at her son's expense. Stephen was still wrestling with some basic literacy skills and didn't handle pressure well. His sense of organization was erratic, and his academic self-confidence was still quite fragile.

At the same time as Stephen's mother was anxious about her son's chances of success in the high school, she was adamant that Stephen would not receive learning support from a special education teacher. She did not want her son labeled as LD (learning disabled); nor did she want her son in a resource room with "those kinds of students" (by which she meant "failures" and "troublemakers").

Stephen's eighth-grade teachers were very concerned that his mother's combination of fear and obstinacy would make the upcoming parent-teacher conference difficult and perhaps even counterproductive. Accordingly, the teachers met together before the conference to plan their approach. Initially, they focused on the negative and highly emotive behavior they expected from Stephen's mother. This led to mutual commiseration in terms of how difficult the conference was going to be but did not provide them with a plan of action. The turning point came when one of the teachers announced that they needed to find "common ground." In other words, they needed to find some important belief or value that all of them, including Stephen's mom, could agree on without qualification. One of the teachers suggested that they all cared deeply about Stephen and wanted to ensure his success in the high school. The teachers agreed that whenever the conference with Stephen's mom became difficult or emotionally fraught, the teachers would return to their common ground—how much they cared for Stephen and how they were all planning for his success in the high school.

With this as their sole strategy, the teachers went into the conference with Stephen's mom. As they predicted, she was both very fearful and very obstinate. However, the teachers were patient and empathetic, returning frequently to their agreed common ground, and by the end of the conference, Stephen's mother had agreed to have Stephen receive special education support in the high school. Part of her turnaround had to do with the fact that Stephen had had a good year in grade eight and she trusted his teachers, but also a large part of the success of the conference was due to the empathy that the teachers exhibited for this very distraught mother. It was conversation filled with emotional intelligence.

WHAT IS EMOTIONAL INTELLIGENCE?

What is emotional intelligence, and why should it be important to a teacher in a classroom? Mayer and Salovey (1997) define emotional intelligence (EQ) as "the ability to perceive accurately, appraise, and express emotion; the ability to access and/or generate feelings when they facilitate thought; the ability to understand emotion and emotional knowledge; and the ability to regulate emotions to promote emotional and intellectual growth" (p. 10). A leading researcher in the area of emotional intelligence in the workplace defines it as a skill through which employees treat emotions as valuable data in navigating a specific situation (Barsade & Gibson, 2007).

Goleman (2006) takes issue with these behavioral definitions of EQ because he finds them devoid of values. In other words, if EQ is simply social acuity and aligned behaviors, it can be employed for all sorts of self-serving, manipulative purposes from selling second-hand cars to confidence games to predatory sexual advances. Goleman rejects the idea that such Machiavellian use of interpersonal skills can be considered "intelligent." He suggests that such trust-destroying behaviors contradict the notion of genuine intelligence, and therefore, he perceives that compassion and caring and other "other-centered" values are inherent in EQ. We share Goleman's perspective.

Daniel Goleman's model of emotional intelligence has been through a number of iterations and we summarize it here based on his original work (1995) and his later books and essays, most notably his work in linking emotional intelligence to the work of leadership (1998, 2001). Goleman suggests five dimensions of emotional intelligence:

1. *Self-knowledge.* People who are emotionally intelligent have a reasonable degree of self-knowledge and are always seeking ways in which they can come to know themselves in deeper, more meaningful ways.

They try to be honest with themselves, balancing their need for self-esteem with their desire for candid feedback from other people. Self-knowledgeable people have a vocabulary for their emotions and tend to feel comfortable within their own skin. They recognize their strengths and weaknesses and treat failure as an opportunity to learn.

People who are unable to know their feelings are at a tremendous disadvantage. "In a sense, they are emotionally illiterate, oblivious to a realm of reality that is crucial for success in life as a whole, let alone work" (Goleman, 1998, p. 66).

2. Self-management and self-regulation. Steven Covey (2004) suggests that humans are the only species that can create distance between the stimulus and their response. In animals, the stimulus is directly followed by the response. When Pavlov rang his bell, his dogs salivated. However, in humans there is the "arena of consciousness," that is, the distance we can choose to create between the stimulus and the response. The arena of consciousness is where we can itemize and analyze our response behaviors. Will I smile coyly or burst into laughter? Will I offer a gentle probing question or blurt out a sarcastic retort? Which response will be most effective in achieving my aims in the given circumstances? It is in this arena of consciousness that we identify our intentions and then manage and regulate our behavior to that end. In the stressful environment of the classroom, the various ways that teachers manage their emotions becomes critically important. This will be explored in some depth in Chapter 4.

3. Motivation. Motivation is the energy source of our labor. Individuals who have lost motivation are often perceived as apathetic, uninterested, depressed, and lethargic. On the other hand, motivated teachers are seen as enthusiastic, efficacious, optimistic, and energetic. The question as to what motivates us to teach strikes at the very heart of our professional self-knowledge.

4. Social awareness. Social awareness is the process of placing ourselves in relationships with others so that we are not only aware of what we are experiencing but also have the *mindsight* (a term that psychologists are increasingly using to describe an intuitive awareness of the thoughts and feelings of others) to understand what others may be experiencing. Recent conjecture (Iacoboni, 2008) suggests that as a species we may have a genetic disposition toward social awareness. In evolutionary terms, it may be that our enhanced ability (over other animal species) to "read" the emotions of others led to an instinct for cooperation. Certainly one of the most distinguishing features of Homo sapiens, as opposed to other animal species, is our predilection for group work and social awareness.

5. *Relationship management.* Often when we listen to young children describe their friendships, it is almost as though these relationships happen to them. They do not necessarily see themselves as the authors or architects of such relationships. On occasion, we hear the same lack of interpersonal efficacy when adults describe a recent divorce or conflict. Either the blame for the fractured relationship is placed on the shoulders of some other person or is assigned to some vague incompatibility or "bad chemistry." As children grow older they become increasingly aware of their investment in and contribution to their relationships. They literally learn how to manage social interactions. Researchers (Brooks & Goldstein, 2001) into so-called resilient children (children who face overwhelming adversity—physical and sexual abuse, neglect, and even abandonment—but still manage to grow into intelligent, compassionate adults) have identified that these children share the belief that *relationships are repairable.* It is this interpersonal efficacy that lies at the very heart of relationship management.

In summary, we start out by perceiving emotions in self and others. This is the degree to which we are capable of attending to emotions, expressing those emotions, and reading the emotions of others. Some teachers seem to have a natural talent for being emotionally sensitive both to self and others. For other teachers, emotional sensitivity is very much a learning process.

From perceiving emotions, we move toward using emotions—the process of knowing which emotions facilitate relationship building effectively and which need to be regulated and controlled. Using emotions implies that we have come to have an understanding of these feelings—the understanding of complicated emotional dynamics, including how emotions can change from one to the other in a very short period of time (e.g., embarrassment to anger). In the next section, we will explore why teachers need to be emotionally intelligent.

WHY TEACHERS NEED EQ

We teach with our emotions as well as our words.

—Ambrizeth Lima in Sonia Nieto (2005, p. 91),
paraphrasing Paulo Freire (1998)

Emotionally intelligent teachers understand that learning is a voluntary act on the part of the learner. Neither teacher nor parent can compel it to happen as much as we might like to. In our well-meaning efforts to force learning onto students, we have sometimes used destructive or coercive strategies, including the use of fear, shame, guilt, and blackmail. We have also held out the enticement of extrinsic rewards, such as grades or gold stars or parental approval or even entrance to prestigious universities.

No matter how we may have attempted to manipulate students into learning, the ultimate decision about whether our students will learn is not ours to make. It is the learner's decision. This speaks to the pithy quotation from Churchill that begins this chapter: "I am always ready to learn although I do not always like being taught." When we use compulsion, students often do not like being taught.

There are some important implications here. First, *teaching* may not be the same as the *facilitation of learning*. Ralph Tyler (1949) recognized this more than fifty years ago when he wrote that "saying 'I taught them, they just didn't learn it' was as foolish as saying 'I sold it to them, they just didn't buy it'" (as cited in Guskey, 2000, pp. 5–7). The teacher can create conditions for learning but can never make the decision to learn for someone else. Just as a skilled gardener can sow seeds, fertilize the ground, and water the seedlings but cannot create plant life; so the teacher can foster the conditions for learning but can't compel the learning to occur. Emotionally intelligent teachers are more able to foster those classroom conditions that maximize the desire to learn on the part of the student.

Learning is forever dependent on relationships and social context. One of the most important relationships is the one between teacher and student. John Medina (2008) writes, "Our ability to learn has deep roots in relationships. . . . Our learning performance may be deeply affected by the emotional environment in which the learning takes place" (p. 45). Without emotional understanding, teachers are likely to experience emotional misunderstanding. This can often be the product of mistaking my feelings for the feelings of others (Denzin, 1984).

Research shows that there is too often a strained or even adversarial relationship between students and teachers. In 2001, a nationwide survey in the United States (*MetLife Survey of the American Teacher*, as cited in Cushman, 2003) found that 65 percent of the students questioned believed that "My teachers don't understand me" (p. 6), and 33 percent of teachers reported inadequate preparation to reach students with cultural backgrounds different from their own. Emotionally intelligent teachers are better able to bridge the "us and them" gulf that permeates so many classrooms.

Teachers with a higher degree of EQ also understand that moods affect our perceptions. For example, if I go to work one day in an irritable mood, I am more likely to discover colleagues who are also in irritable moods than if I entered the workplace cheerful and relaxed. Forthcoming chapters will examine in some depth how we identify our own emotions and those of others and how emotions can be highly contagious.

The importance of emotional intelligence in the classroom is that it fosters a high degree of accuracy in emotional understanding. This, in turn, fosters relationships based on trust that support student learning.

On the other hand, emotional misunderstanding strikes at the foundation of teaching and learning, lowering standards and depressing quality. Successful teaching and learning, therefore, depend on establishing close bonds with students and on creating teaching conditions that make emotional understanding possible (Hargreaves, 2001). In the traditional classroom, one of the obstacles to developing classroom relationships based upon trust has been the topography of power.

THE POWER TOPOGRAPHY OF THE CLASSROOM

Part and parcel of the emotional landscape of the classroom is the topography of power—the location, distribution, and uses of authority. There is no question that teachers have enormous power over students. For the most part, students have not chosen to be present in our classes. They have been sent and therefore constitute a captive audience. We hold them in a room with a predetermined seating plan for a prescribed period of time every school day, punishing them if they are late or absent without a valid excuse. They need our explicit permission to leave the classroom even to visit the toilet. We determine what activities they will engage in. We determine the rules of behavior that they will abide by. We even determine if and when they will be allowed to speak. When you think about it, there are few environments as restrictive as the classroom.

For the teacher, this "power topography" brings with it the profound responsibility to use it appropriately (D. Jensen, 2004). Stephen Gordon (as cited in Nieto, 2005) eloquently sums up that responsibility by defining the teacher's responsibility to make the classroom a "sacred, life-affirming place" (p. 80). The power topography of the classroom makes relationship building between the teacher and students problematic and further underscores the critical importance of teacher emotional intelligence.

In our experience, the power topography of the classroom is largely determined by the teacher's assumptions about the ultimate purpose and goal of the classroom experience. The power topography becomes pronounced when the teacher's goal is student compliance and conformity. On the other hand, the negative implications of the power topography are vastly diminished when the teacher's goal is to facilitate learning, and classroom management becomes simply a means to that end. There is a subtle but significant difference here, and the distinction requires teacher emotional intelligence.

TEACHERS AS MANAGERS OF EMOTION

Emotionally intelligent teachers are aware of their emotions as they experience them. A recent meta-analysis of research reported a positive relationship between greater accuracy in emotion recognition and better work outcomes in occupations as diverse as physicians, medical interns, human service workers, foreign service officers, principals, schoolteachers, and business executives (Elfenbein, Foo, White, Tan, & Aik, 2007). However, emotional awareness is not sufficient in and of itself.

As teachers, we need to understand the separate, but related, components of emotional intelligence. For example, two teachers may both be excellent readers of emotion in others. However, if one is better at regulating how emotions affect behavior, this individual may be perceived as more predictable and therefore trustworthy in the classroom. This may make the latter's classroom a more effective learning environment.

Emotionally intelligent teachers understand that emotions and cognition are inseparably merged in the process of learning, especially learning something that is new and challenging. There is no divide between the heart and the head or between the body and the mind (Pert, 1997).

CLASSROOM STRESS AND LEARNING

Teachers need emotional intelligence in order to deal with classroom stress—their own and their students'. Teachers with high EQ create classrooms that are physically and psychologically safe. If children are frightened about their physical safety (e.g., being beaten up after school, being bullied on the playground, being sexually harassed in the hallways) their learning will be dramatically impeded. The same is true when children feel psychologically threatened: when their self-esteem is undermined, when they perceive that they are low status in comparison with classmates, or when they feel excluded or alienated from a peer group.

When students feel psychologically threatened in a classroom, powerful chemicals are released in the body and brain. These are the so-called stress chemicals: cortisol and adrenaline. The most common reaction to a flood of these chemicals is *fight, flight,* or *freeze.* The differing responses depend greatly on the child's temperament and self-confidence, but it is probably fair to say that most psychologically threatened children initially freeze like a jackrabbit in the headlights of a car. The neocortex shuts down, and any prospect of learning is abandoned. Psychological threat (fear of criticism, ridicule or humiliation, or exclusion from the group) doesn't just affect the present moment but remains as an impediment to learning for a significant length of time.

Experience suggests that teachers can also be subject to acute and chronic stress. Part of this stress comes from the nature of our work with children. Teachers make between four hundred and one thousand decisions in the course of an average day in the classroom. Most of these decisions are in-the-moment choices. They are spontaneous, and there is no time for thoughtful reflection. Even when decisions require careful thought, teachers have little opportunity for prolonged concentration. Their days are a barrage of urgent interruptions. For these reasons, Millet and others (2005) place teaching in the top seven most stressful occupations. Perhaps it is no wonder that 60 percent of beginning teachers leave the profession within the first five years. Teaching requires an intense degree of emotional labor.

It is our contention that teachers with high degrees of emotional intelligence (EQ) cope with stress much more effectively than those with limited EQ. The latter tend to make classrooms anxiety filled for their students and themselves.

Neuroscience is replete with research on how anxiety and stress affect the brain. In his book *Why Zebras Don't Get Ulcers,* Robert Sapolsky (2004) points out that the body's chemical responses to stress are superbly matched to a brief, mad dash away from a hungry lion on the African savannah. However, such chemical responses are much less appropriate when the stressors become chronic and long lasting and we worry and fret for months on end about problems at work, marital difficulties, or financial matters. It is chronic and prolonged stress that can be damaging to both our psychological and physical health. A stressor is anything in the external world that "knocks" a person out of homeostatic balance (Sapolsky). The geography of teaching is full of such potentially chronic stressors—behind every rock and tree there is . . . well perhaps not a hungry lion but certainly the impulsive student in the back of the class who has just stuck a bean as far as possible up one nostril, the new child who uses English as a second language and who hasn't said a word all week, the sullen colleague with whom you are expected to collaborate, that never-ending pile of paperwork that someone irritatingly reminds you is *urgent,* and the parent of the frightfully gifted student who holds you personally responsible for the child's ennui. Anyone who doesn't believe that teaching is stressful has never tried it.

Stress can result in an amygdala hijacking of the neocortex, which results in "downshifting"—a paralysis of executive functioning—such as Bill suffered as a child when trying to solve a simple arithmetic problem in front of the class. A stressed teacher can produce a stressful classroom, and this can be a major obstacle to student learning.

Recent research suggests that stress responses can be gender specific and that the fight, flight, or freeze response is more common in males than females. Psychologist Shelley Taylor (2006) from UCLA suggests that the physiology of the stress response can be quite different in females. She argues that in most species females are typically less aggressive than males and that being the primary caregiver for her offspring precludes the option of flight. Taylor suggests that the female stress response may be more along the lines of "tend and befriend." This has interesting implications given the high proportion of women who teach primary schoolchildren.

Not all stress is negatively correlated to learning. Occasional or moderate stress can actually enhance learning. We refer to this type of stress as *eustress*. The term was coined by the endocrinologist Hans Selye (1975) to describe stress associated with fulfillment or positive feelings as opposed to the negative and harmful *distress*.

Emotionally intelligent teachers are able to "read" the stress landscape of the classroom. They understand that the degree of challenge of the learning experience can provide students with either eustress or distress. What makes the difference is whether the challenge is appropriate for the learner's readiness level. To optimize learning, students need to be working in their zone of proximal development (Vygotsky, 1978), where the challenge is appropriately matched to their readiness level. This is a level of challenge on the frontier between tasks that are too easy and therefore boring and activities that are too difficult and complex and therefore meaningless or paralytically stressful. When children are in their zone of proximal development, they are accomplishing tasks with adult support and guidance—tasks that they probably would not be able to undertake independently.

Teachers with high EQ appreciate that there is a relationship between healthy stress and the degree of student control involved. If the student has some degree of control over the challenge (the challenge is in part set by the student or the student has a degree of choice), stress can produce self-confidence, efficacy, and resilience. However, prolonged, high levels of stress can be debilitating. Chronic stress over time kills brain cells, reduces new brain cell production, impairs the immune system, damages the hippocampus, and causes an atrophy of dendrites (E. Jensen, 2005). Prolonged and chronic stress release corticosteroids which reduce blood flow in the top of the frontal lobes—an area of the brain responsible for "on your feet" thinking. To maximize learning for all students, emotionally intelligent teachers are aware of the individual and collective emotional reactions of their students.

However, before we can be emotionally sensitive to our students, we need to be emotionally sensitive to ourselves. We need to embark on the inner journey of knowing our own emotional landscapes.

2 The Inner Journey

Knowing Ourselves as Teachers

You don't see something until you have the right metaphor to let you perceive it.

—Thomas Kuhn (1962, p. 112)

THE "SO WHAT?" QUESTION

A few years ago, a British elementary schoolteacher told us a story about herself that illustrates a powerful aspect of how self-knowledge can be central to effective teaching. Bernie (B. Williams, personal communication, 2005) was working with her fifth-grade class on writing short, descriptive passages. She had the students write paragraphs about a memory that was particularly important to them. The students were able to do this with relative ease, but Bernie wanted to take them to a deeper level by asking them the "So what?" question. She wanted her students to distill the essence of their memory writing and synthesize the meaning it had for them. She wanted them to uncover insights and perhaps even frame new concepts or generalizations about themselves. Although she did not describe it as such, Bernie was attempting to engage her young students in one of the most cognitively demanding, challenging aspects of writing: framing a meaningful conclusion.

Bernie struggled with this for several weeks. She recognized that what she was attempting was challenging for her young students, and she even wondered whether they were developmentally ready for what she was asking of them.

In an attempt to illustrate what she was looking for, Bernie decided to write her own "memory piece" and share it with her class. She wrote a short piece about how on one Saturday several years before, she and her own children had spontaneously gone shopping for a pet and had purchased a puppy. As she read the piece to her class, her eyes became moist and her voice wavered with emotion. "You could hear a pin drop," she recalled. When she finished reading there was silence, broken finally when a student said, "Ms. Bernie, you look like you're going to cry."

Bernie recalled that moment as a critical juncture. "I was ready to cry, and my British reserve told me that was entirely inappropriate. But something intuitively told me that I needed to share my emotional response with the class. Later that evening, it came to me. In reading my memory piece to the class, I had answered the 'So what?' question. I had written about how small, seemingly insignificant events can be tremendously important in building a mother-child relationship. Shopping for that puppy had refreshed my love affair with motherhood. The next day, I explained this to the class and described how writing and reading this paragraph had helped me to construct new insight into myself. In front of the class, I added a final sentence that captured the emotional essence of my story. Not all the students were able to understand what I was talking about, but a few were, and their writing improved dramatically."

In this short classroom vignette, Bernie not only illustrated the meaning that can be derived from writing, but she modeled for her students how adults handle powerful emotions. She sent the message that emotions were permissible in the classroom. They were not something that we need to be frightened or ashamed of. She also modeled the acquisition of self-knowledge in a powerful way. From her self-disclosure, the students witnessed not only how writing can reveal emotional relevance but how adults, no less than children, are constantly engaged in learning about who they are. This was an emotionally intelligent interchange.

KNOWING OURSELVES THROUGH REFLECTION

Professional self-knowledge is crucial to teacher effectiveness in the classroom. The teacher creates important learning relationships with students either consciously or subconsciously. These learning relationships are the social and emotional bedrock of effective teacher and student learning. When these relationships are consciously and reflectively constructed, instruction is enhanced for all students, especially for struggling learners.

The key to uncovering professional self-knowledge is reflection.

Someone once said that humankind does not learn by experience but rather by reflection upon experience. There is an important distinction. Experience happens to us; reflection, on the other hand, is the process through which we attempt to make sense out of experience. Reflection is emotion and experience recollected and processed in tranquility. When Bernie *intuitively* knew that she needed to share her emotional response to her piece of writing with her students, she was acting on a hunch. She had not planned this. Bernie was doing what many highly experienced teachers do—she was trusting in her subconscious mind to make decisions. The chances are that if you had interrupted Bernie's lesson and asked her why she was sharing her own emotional reaction with the class, she would have given you a blank stare—unable, on the spot, to verbalize the rationale for her decision making. However, given time and tranquility (later that night) Bernie was able to reflect on the big picture—to perceive how her example of emotional relevance modeled for the students how to address the "So what?" question. Reflection allowed Bernie to make meaning out of experience.

When the subject of reflection comes up in conversations with teachers, the most common response is to question where on earth the time will come from. Increasingly, our professional lives seem like a perpetual rush hour, and we seem like the steel balls in a hyperactive pinball machine bouncing from urgency to urgency, with a great deal of sound and fury but not much time for the making of meaning. "Where is the time?" is a good question but inadequately framed. Time is not a commodity that we can buy, rent, beg, borrow, or steal. What we can do, however, is to rethink our priorities for the use of our precious professional time. If it is true that we do not learn from experience, but from reflection on experience, there can be no greater priority in teacher professional development than time given over for *structured* and *rigorous professional* reflection.

Becoming aware of one's own emotional life in the classroom is not necessarily a naturally occurring phenomenon. In fact, in many cases it is a conscious act of professional willpower. It requires almost an out-of-body experience where we disengage emotionally from a situation and observe as an interested but unreactive witness. Goleman (2006) writes that "people in the helping professions must work hard to ensure that the ingredients of rapport operate during professional encounters. Their detachment needs to be balanced with sufficient empathy to allow at least a bit of I-You feeling to bloom" (p. 112). We need to combine rapport with a macrocentric vision. A helpful metaphor for this temporary emotional detachment may be taking the "balcony view," when we deliberately remove ourselves from the emotional moment and take a climb to a metaphoric balcony to gain distance from and perspective on the situation.

Without this detachment, we may be unaware of how students are interpreting our behavior. Alexis (Cushman, 2003), a high school student, writes about how teachers are perceived to give more attention to some students than to others. She sees teachers giving more of themselves to students who succeed than those who fail. The message for Alexis is clear. She is not worth the teacher's time because there are other students with more potential than she has.

Comprehending ourselves emotionally is nothing short of understanding the world we live in. We must be able to recognize our emotions and possess a vocabulary for them in order to understand not only self but others and, in fact, the world around us.

Goleman (2006) writes that self-awareness seems to require an "activated neocortex, particularly the language areas, attuned to identify and name the emotions being aroused" (p. 47). An emotion that is named is one that is consciously identified. The act of identification serves to provide us psychological distance from the overwhelming power of that emotion. An Anglican minister friend of ours is fond of saying that the greatest gift that parents and teachers can give children is a vocabulary for their emotions. If we can put into words what we are feeling, we can gain some disengagement from it, escape some of its tyrannical influence, and so become its author and architect. Recent research (Hariri, Bookheimer, & Mazziotta, 2000, as cited in Goleman) suggests that there may be a neurological basis for this phenomenon—that the cognitive process involved in the labeling of an emotion actually disrupts affect-related amygdala activity.

Teachers, like everyone else, are subject to moods. While a few may assume that negative teacher moods will never enter the classroom, such an expectation is as unrealistic as expecting students to leave their emotional lives outside the schoolhouse. However, self-aware individuals are cognizant of their moods *as they are having them*. They are able to identify and label negative moods so as not to fixate upon them. As a result, they are able to get out of them sooner.

Moods tend to last longer than emotions and generally are not connected to a single event in our environment. In many cases, moods occur for reasons that the person experiencing the mood does not understand. Moods may well be generated by neurohormonal changes. Paul Ekman (Dalai Lama & Ekman, 2008) suggests that moods can trigger emotions:

When we are in an apprehensive mood we are looking to be afraid. We are responding to the world with fear more than anything else, often misperceiving the world. It is as if we *need* to be afraid when we are in an apprehensive mood, just like we *need* to get angry when we are in an irritable mood. (p. 9)

Our moods color our perceptions. They filter what we see and hear of the world and make us respond to a distorted view of reality. Ekman (Dalai Lama & Ekman, 2008) suggests that when we are undergoing a mood, particularly a negative mood such as anxiety, anger, or irritation, we enter a refractory period during which we tend only to process and remember information that fits the given mood.

However, teachers with a high degree of emotional self-awareness can recognize the connection between the mood they are experiencing and what they think, say, and do. They realize the powerful impact of moods on behavior and can achieve the detachment necessary to transform them.

In order for teachers to know themselves, they need to keep a finger on their emotional pulse. However, we cannot separate emotional and cognitive lives. Therefore, it is also important for teachers to know themselves as learners.

MY WAY OR THE HIGHWAY: KNOWING OURSELVES AS LEARNERS

Many teachers, particularly beginning teachers just embarking on a career in education, are subject to a variation of what social psychologist Lee Ross (1977) labeled the *fundamental attribution error* (FAE): "FAE refers to a general human tendency to overestimate the importance of personality or dispositional factors relative to situational or environmental influences when describing and explaining the causes of social behavior" (as cited in Aronson, 2008, p. 164). The FAE variation that we see in some educators is the unexamined presumption that "the manner in which I learn most efficiently is the manner in which *other people* learn most efficiently." Because, until relatively recently, individual learning styles and intelligence preferences were not a subject of direct, critical study, teachers had little option but to look to their own past learning experiences for models of effectiveness. In a one-size-fits-all world, this would work nicely. The basic misconception here is that we don't live in such a homogenous or simple world.

The fact that different people learn differently is often a very hard concept for teachers to grasp. On occasion in our workshops on differentiation, a teacher will complain about an activity (perhaps a kinesthetic or tactual exercise) that didn't match his or her particular learning style. They are often surprised and taken aback when they come to realize that the activity "worked" for other teachers in the group.

Knowing our own learning styles provides a window into the different learning styles of others. Many teachers start their journey of self-exploration by posing questions to themselves about whether they are primarily visual, auditory, tactual, or kinesthetic learners. They recall a particularly effective (or ineffective) teacher from their past and analyze the match or mismatch between the teaching and their own learning style. They observe themselves when they concentrate most deeply. What are the environmental factors? Is there music in the background? Have they selected hard or soft furniture? Are they alone or part of a group conversation? Do they work for long stretches or do they require frequent breaks? By self-examination, we come to understand the multiplicity of factors that contribute to learning efficiency and so decrease the likelihood that we will impose our preferred learning style on our students as a monotonous pedagogical diet.

Fortunately, most of us are not pure types when it comes to learning, and therefore, we intuitively appreciate the need for instructional diversity. However, it is important to remember that most people who enter the teaching profession were themselves successful at school, suggesting that teachers generally tend to have reasonably high preferences for linguistic and logical-mathematical intelligences, those intelligences which are most often recognized and rewarded in schools. Teachers also tend (as does the general population at large) toward being visual learners. Also reflecting the general population, not many teachers are strong auditory or kinesthetic learners. This becomes powerfully significant when we recognize that a significant proportion of boys with learning disabilities prefer kinesthetic or tactual learning experiences.

When Bill is interviewing teachers for employment, he will often ask them about their preferred learning styles and about their own experiences as students. Often those teachers who struggled in school, failed classes, were retained in a grade, or even dropped out of high school exhibit a greater degree of knowledge of themselves as learners than those for whom school success came easily. Those who struggled in school often exhibit greater empathy for those for whom learning is a challenge.

HIGHLY EFFECTIVE TEACHERS AND EMOTIONAL SELF-KNOWLEDGE

A synthesis of research (Nieto, 2005) suggests a number of common characteristics that describe highly effective teachers. In addition to strong subject-matter knowledge, pedagogical effectiveness, and excellent communication skills, highly effective teachers were seen to be emotionally self-aware in that they exhibited the following characteristics—all of which demand considerable emotional intelligence. As you read through the list below, attempt to identify the emotional awareness that is required. For example, for teachers to connect to student lives, they probably engage in a degree of self-conscious empathy. When teachers challenge the school's bureaucracy, it is often because they have become aware of a conflict between the way the school is operating and their deeply held professional values and beliefs.

Highly effective teachers

- Connect learning to students' lives
- Have high expectations for all students, even for those whom others may have given up on
- Stay committed to students in spite of obstacles that get in the way
- Place a high value on students' identities (culture, race, language, gender, and experiences, among others) as a foundation for learning
- View parents and other community members as partners in education
- Create a safe haven for learning
- Dare to challenge the bureaucracy of the school
- Are resilient in the face of difficult situations
- Use active learning strategies
- Are willing and eager to experiment and can "think on their feet"
- View themselves as lifelong learners
- Care about, respect, and love their students (Nieto, 2005, p. 9)

Reflection is the key to emotional self-knowledge, but it is often extremely challenging when undertaken in solitude. Some of the most meaningful reflection takes place between trusting colleagues, as the story of Diana illustrates.

DIANA AND THE WHINY GIRLS

Diana (D. Mahon, personal communication, 2006) was a fourth-grade teacher who had come to her principal with a problem. She was increasingly finding herself irritated and short tempered with a group of "whiny" girls in her class. Diana didn't like her emotional response to the girls and recognized that it was counterproductive but didn't understand where it was coming from within herself. Her principal coached Diana, paraphrased her concerns, and probed for specificity and clarity. Diana came to recognize that the whiny behavior of the girls was clashing with her own feminist values. "They are stereotypic of disempowered young women everywhere." Diana wanted the girls to exhibit greater efficacy and self-confidence. The coaching conversation with her principal allowed Diana to explore her own deeply held values and analyze the classroom interaction. She was able to emotionally disengage and take the "balcony" view. She and her principal explored ways in which she could help the group of girls find the inner resource of efficacy.

Diana's introspection allowed her to move from being reactive to proactive. She was able to see that while her feelings of irritation may have had a negative impact on classroom interaction, these feelings were motivated by powerful positive values. She could now focus on supporting the girls without allowing them to "push her buttons." In gaining professional self-knowledge she created the potential for many learning opportunities in her classroom.

However, self-awareness is not the same thing as skill in social interaction. We have all met socially awkward or shy individuals who were painfully aware that they were socially inept but were seemingly unable to do anything about it.

There is a significant difference between *declarative knowledge,* knowing intellectually what the ideas and concepts are, and *procedural knowledge,* possessing the skills and dispositions to actually be able to do something or modify our behavior accordingly. In the classroom situation where we are charged with the responsibility for constructing positive learning relationships with our students, declarative knowledge by itself is obviously insufficient. Knowing what learning relationships we would like to create but not having the tools to develop them is clearly a recipe for frustration and impotence. However, emotional self-awareness is unquestionably the starting point.

Teachers with high degrees of emotional self-awareness know their strengths and their limits. They have an accurate appraisal of their respective talents and weaknesses. They are reflective and are able to learn from experience. They take responsible risks, and when they fail, they "fail forward" and treat the incident as an opportunity for growth and learning. Such teachers solicit and value candid feedback from colleagues, supervisors, students, and parents. They are open to new perspectives and see themselves on a continuous journey of self-development. Teachers with a high degree of self-awareness are also able to demonstrate an appropriate sense of humor and laugh at themselves.

THE CIRCUITRY FOR LAUGHTER: HUMOR AND SELF-AWARENESS

The role of humor in the emotionally intelligent classroom is worth a moment's pause. Bill has recruited teachers for international schools for the past twenty-five years, and he has never knowingly hired a teacher without a sense of humor. For Bill, an appropriate sense of humor ranks very high among the attributes of the high-quality teacher.

The great eighteenth-century philosopher Immanuel Kant (as cited in Ayan, 2009) counted laughter among the triad of strategies that allow humans to face the tribulations of daily life (the other two were *hope* and *sleep*).

Why is appropriate humor so important in the classroom? There are several ways to address the question. First of all, when we say *appropriate* humor, we are talking about the type of humor in which everyone is able to laugh *with* everyone else. We are not talking about laughing *at* an individual or the type of humor that humiliates, ridicules, or alienates.

Humor can be a powerful bonding agent in the classroom. For example, when a teacher pokes gentle fun at himself, the students perceive an adult who has self-knowledge and is honest and courageous enough to engage in a degree of self-disclosure. This openness is often much appreciated by students.

There is also a strong relationship between humor and our response to stress. Humor often involves a sudden shift in perspectives, a paradigm or a logical shift. For example, there was this joke going around the Internet a few months ago . . .

AN ATHEIST IN THE WOODS

An atheist went out for a walk in the forest. He came through a small clearing in the trees and was confronted by an enormous grizzly bear. The bear charged forward to attack. The terrified atheist turned to run but tripped and fell to the ground. The menacing bear came in for the kill, reaching for him with his left paw and raising his right paw to strike him!

And in that instant, the atheist cried out: "Oh my God!"

Time stopped. The bear froze. The forest was silent. As an enormous shaft of golden light came down from Heaven, and a mighty voice said: "You deny my existence for all these years, teach others that I don't exist, and even suggest that creation was a cosmic accident. Do you really expect me to help you now? Am I to count you among the believers?"

The atheist looked directly into the light. "It would be hypocritical of me to suddenly ask you to treat me as a Christian, but perhaps you could make the bear a Christian."

"Very well," the voice said.

The golden light went out and the forest noises resumed. And the bear dropped its right paw, brought both its paws together, bowed its head and spoke: "For this food I am about to receive may the Lord make me truly thankful . . ." (An Atheist in the Woods, 2007, p. 1)

The ambiguity of perspectives makes the story amusing to both believers and nonbelievers. It can be understood at a number of different levels. A sudden shift in perspective stimulates the brain, and the laughter can serve as a tonic to stress.

Clinical psychologist Michael Titze, founder of HumorCare, an organization that promotes humor as a form of therapy, believes that the humorous perspective creates cognitive distance between oneself and the obstacles and challenges we face and as such can be psychologically protective (Ayan, 2009). Other studies have shown that subjects who had been engaged in laughter at a funny film showed lower concentrations of the stress hormone cortisol in their blood. This brings us to the classroom connection between humor and stress.

By definition, a highly effective classroom is a stressful place. It is stressful in a number of different ways. First, it is stressful for students because they are being challenged appropriately. They are working within their zone of proximal development on tasks that make them a little uncomfortable because they are not yet able to complete these challenges independently. They are being called upon to take intellectual and emotional risks. The effective classroom is also stressful for the teacher, who is constantly observing, monitoring, revising, and adapting lessons to meet the needs of students. The teacher is intellectually and emotionally invested in the achievement of students. An appropriate degree of humor can actually take the edge off this stress.

We are not suggesting that teachers need to master the skills of a stand-up comic. However, the effective teacher is cheerful and, on occasion, playful. Having a lighthearted interaction style facilitates bonding with students and builds social support networks. Another benefit of humor and cheerfulness is resilience—a psychic buoyancy in the face of defeat or major disappointment. Appropriate classroom humor promotes the resilience of both the teacher and the students.

Stress is necessary in the high-quality classroom, but it must not be unrelenting. Prolonged emotional stress (such as can be produced by repeated failure) can result in the chemical cortisol attacking the neurons of the hippocampus, slowing neuron growth, or actually atrophying the existing neurons. The hippocampus is the part of the brain responsible for the conversion of "working memory" into long-term memory. If it is impaired, there is a profoundly negative effect on memory and learning.

Both students and teachers need periodic, regular relief from stress, and this is where humor and a sense of playfulness become critical. Jaak Panksepp (Goleman, 2006) from Bowling Green State University notes that all young mammals engage in spirited playfulness—rough-and-tumble play—whether they are puppies, lion cubs, or kindergarteners. He suggests that subcortical circuitry that prompts this playfulness appears to have an important role in development of a child's neural growth. Periodic playfulness in the classroom can actually serve to reinforce the seriousness of the serious.

The circuitry for laughter resides in the oldest and most primitive part of the brain, the brain stem—which suggests that humor may have played an important role in our evolution as a species, serving perhaps as the social glue that bound small kinship groups together in cooperative hunting and gathering activities, giving rise to community and ultimately to culture. Laughter serves exactly the same bonding purpose in the classroom. It gives rise to the specific climatic signature of the classroom. Goleman (2006) writes that "laughter may be the shortest distance between two brains, an unstoppable infectious spread that builds an instant social bond" (p. 45).

Self-knowledge can also serve to promote professional self-confidence. This can produce what we refer to as "presence."

A TEACHER WITH "PRESENCE"

Most schools have witnessed the following scenario. A teacher is ill, and a substitute teacher is called in for the day. The substitute teacher is unfamiliar with the class and perhaps also with the subject area. The insecurity of the novice is communicated to the students nonverbally, and they in turn decide to act out and test the limits of the substitute's authority. The substitute passes out a sign-up sheet to take attendance, and it comes back to him bearing the signatures of "Mickey Mouse," "Frank Purdue," and "A. N. Other."

The substitute struggles to maintain order and classroom decorum. However, despite the best of efforts, the children's behavior is increasingly off the wall. The chaos continues until the noise level reaches such a volume that the next-door teacher appears to find out what is going on. The next-door teacher, a veteran, stands in the doorway, hands on hips, and stares at the misbehaving students. For several moments, not a word is spoken. Slowly, all the students fall silent. The veteran teacher announces, "You will all return to your seats, now." And to the astonishment of the substitute teacher, the students do as they are instructed.

Later, after the end of the school day, the substitute asks the veteran, "How did you do that?" The veteran shrugs and replies, "It's just something you learn from experience."

The veteran teacher has "presence." What is this presence that can restore order out of chaos without uttering a word?

Having a powerful emotional presence is closely allied to emotional self-awareness. It comes from a sense of sureness about one's self-worth and competence. The teacher with presence demonstrates congruence between verbal and nonverbal behavior. What is said and what is done are complementary. There is consistency and a strong degree of predictability in the classroom.

The teacher with presence is a master at using the two "teacher voices." Teachers tend to use two types of voices in the classroom: the credible voice and the approachable voice.

The credible voice is the voice of authority. It is the voice we use when giving instructions or establishing class routines. It has only a small degree of modulation and it tends to curl down at the end of the sentence. *Would you please sit down, now.*

The approachable voice is invitational. Early childhood teachers are masters of the approachable voice. It has considerable modulation and curls up at the end of the sentence. *Would you like me to read you a story?*

When we want to encourage students to think deeply, we must use the approachable voice. If we use the credible voice, the question will sound like interrogation and will actually shut down thinking.

The intentional use of the credible and approachable voices is so important in the classroom that we believe teachers who fail to master their appropriate use probably leave the profession within a year or two. They are simply unable to manage a classroom. On the other hand, insecure teachers may tend to overuse the credible voice. Self-aware teachers understand the power and the appropriateness of their different voices.

TEACHER DISPOSITIONS

The self-aware teacher also has a good understanding of the dispositions that one brings to the classroom. Dispositions are long-term attitudes and emotional predilections. Lyubomirsky, King, and Diener (2005) conducted a comprehensive research meta-analysis and concluded that an individual's tendency to experience positive emotions and moods is associated with increases in a variety of work performance measures, including more positive supervisory evaluations, higher income, enhanced negotiating ability, and performing discretionary acts for the benefit of the organization. Such can be the power of optimism and hopefulness.

KNOWING OUR CULTURAL BAGGAGE

Just as it is impossible for teachers to leave their emotions outside the schoolhouse, it is just as impossible for them to separate their instructional practices from the culture or cultures that they have grown up in. Our cultural orientation pervades everything we do; it forms a foundation for our values and beliefs and influences our behavior. According to Professor Richard Nisbett (2003), it also determines to some extent our cognitive processes, the way we think. Recent brain scans of Americans and East Asians have confirmed differences in information processing by different cultures (Goldberg, 2008).

The purpose here is not to advocate for a classroom devoid of cultural influence; such would be an impossibility in any case. The objective is simply to provide ourselves with greater awareness of the role that the teacher's culture plays in the construction of professional perceptions and the development of learning relationships.

Many schools in the United States and Western Europe, perhaps even most, are now truly multicultural. Globalization has promoted demographic mobility and increased the cultural diversity of our schools. It is not uncommon to find schools in the United States or the United Kingdom with thirty or forty nationalities represented in their student populations and an equal number of different language groups. It is also very common to have teachers who do not share the cultural background of their students.

The self-aware teacher understands that the cultural baggage brought to the classroom often remains invisible to self, but may be glaringly apparent to multicultural students. For example, Western teachers often expect children who are being scolded to maintain eye contact with them during the admonishment. However, such eye contact would be unthinkable to many Asian children since it would represent insolence and defiance.

The message to the teacher of multicultural children is that we need to become more deeply aware of how our own culture is influencing the decisions we are making about learning in our classrooms. Perhaps the most efficient way of doing this is to examine some of the educational beliefs, values, and practices in other cultures and contrast them with our own. Nisbett (2003), in his provocative and fascinating book *The Geography of Thought,* cites the studies of the Japanese historian Masako Watanabe in terms of how historical events are dealt with differently in Japanese and American classrooms. Nisbett suggests that Western educators and students engage in highly causal attribution, whereas Asian educators and students seem more focused on the background and context of the historical event.

Watanabe (as cited in Nisbett, 2003) further suggests that Western teachers appear to be much more outcome based or goal oriented than Asian teachers. They carry into the classroom with them models of formal reasoning that are remarkably different from their Asian counterparts. She quotes an American instructor of English as a second language as saying, "It is very difficult for American teachers to understand Japanese students' essays because they don't see any causality in them, and . . . the relation of cause and effect is elementary logic in the United States" (p. 128).

Neuroscience research, confirmed by fMRI (functional magnetic resonance imaging), appears to support Nisbett's contention that culture influences the way we think. Medina (2008) suggests that actual neural wiring of the brain is dependent upon individual experience, which is of course culturally influenced. "Our brains are so sensitive to external inputs that their physical wiring depends upon the culture in which they find themselves" (p. 61). Medina goes on to state that our dominant cultural background plays a significant role in determining what we pay attention to.

Many tacit beliefs and presuppositions about learning are products of our cultural heritage and are surprisingly inaccessible to conscious reflection. Jerome Bruner (1996) suggests that cultural presuppositions acquired in childhood may become notoriously automatized and remarkably resistant to reflection and introspection. He offers us as an example the notion that thinking is hard cognitive labor. We tend to take for granted that we and others (our students) are not thinking unless there are accompanying signs of great effort. In the West, rigorous is often equated with onerous (Kusuma-Powell & Powell, 2000). Bruner then invites the reader to compare two images of "thinkers": Rodin's well-known bronze and a wooden Japanese figure of the sixteenth century. Rodin's figure is the embodiment of massive concentration and intensely focused internal mental energy. He almost appears constipated. The Japanese figure, on the other hand, is delicately hesitant, serene, and suggestive of aesthetic contemplation—effortlessness that stands in stark contrast to our Western almost painful concentration.

Bruner (1996) refers to the tacit preconceptions that teachers bring to the classroom as "folk pedagogies" and suggests that they reflect a variety of assumptions about children:

> They may seem willful and needing correction; as innocent and to be protected from a vulgar society; as needing skills to be developed only through practice; as empty vessels to be filled with knowledge that only adults can provide; as egocentric and in need of socialization. Folk beliefs of this kind, whether expressed by lay people or by "experts" badly want some "deconstruction" if their implications are to be appreciated. For whether these assumptions are "right" or not, their impact on teaching activities can be enormous. (p. 49)

Folk pedagogies are assumptions, and we know two important things about assumptions. The first is that they exert a very powerful influence over our belief systems and behavior, and second, most of them are held subconsciously. It is therefore particularly useful for teachers to bring to the conscious mind some of these assumptions about the young people we teach daily (Powell & Kusuma-Powell, 2007a).

THE SELF-AWARE TEACHER: WHAT DO WE BELIEVE ABOUT CHILDREN?

Even the most basic folk pedagogies are in desperate need of deconstruction. Take, for example, the very different ways that teachers perceive childhood. Our perceptions of childhood determine to a considerable degree how we actually interact with the children and young adults in our classes.

Many times, the assumptions that influence these perceptions are held at a subconscious level.

To examine these assumptions, we have developed (Powell & Kusuma-Powell, 2007b) five possible lenses through which childhood can be perceived. These are obviously broad generalizations, and we readily acknowledge that there are other lenses and that no one person is a pure type. However, it is sometimes useful to have such models or lenses before us as we explore the process through which we construct our perceptions.

1. The Hobbesian lens. Named after the seventeenth-century British philosopher Thomas Hobbes, this perspective views education as the process of preparing children to live in a civilized and responsible society. Human nature is understood to be profoundly influenced by selfishness. Through the Hobbesian lens, the moral order of civilized society is something that must be explicitly taught to children. When viewed though this lens, children are seen as potential savages with a leviathan residing within them that must be brought under control. Accordingly, one of the most basic purposes of education is to socialize and domesticate children. Childhood is, thus, a period in which children learn to control their selfish urges and to master their destructive emotions. It is preparation for a responsible life.

At its best, the Hobbesian perception emphasizes that young children should be taught social skills such as taking turns, sharing, empathy, and how to delay gratification. We see the influence of the Hobbesian lens in many of our school missions statements that include the goal of developing young people into "responsible world citizens" or preparing them to "live an ethical life."

When taken to an extreme, the Hobbesian perception of childhood can be dehumanizing and cruel. It characterized a great deal of education during the Victorian era and early twentieth century. Teacher control of the classroom was considered of paramount importance. Children were to be "seen and not heard." Compliance was the order of the day and corporal punishment was routine. The "rod" in Proverbs 13:24 ("He who spareth the rod, hateth his son." King James Version) was clearly interpreted to be the ubiquitous malacca cane that hung next to the teacher's desk, not the consoling rod of the Psalm 23:4 ("Thy rod and thy staff, they comfort me." King James Version). Students were primarily motivated through fear.

Freud's (1930/1989) model of the conscious mind (ego) as a battleground between the bestial, amoral, and pleasure-seeking id and our ever-restraining superego (conscience) can be seen as a permutation of the Hobbesian lens. Young people need to acquire self-control.

We can even see the influence of the Hobbesian perspective in the behaviorism of the 1970s and 1980s. Teachers were heavily influenced by B. F. Skinner's (1971) operant conditioning, and student self-control was to be engineered through the use of positive and negative reinforcements.

One of the most eloquent representations of the Hobbesian perception of childhood is presented in William Golding's classic novel, *The Lord of the Flies* (1954), in which a group of English choirboys are stranded on a deserted island following the crash of their airplane. Unlike the resourceful, resilient, and morally upstanding *Swiss Family Robinson* (Wyss, 1813/2007) or the schoolboy chums of *Coral Island* (Ballantyne, 1857, from whence Golding took his inspiration), Golding's choir boys descend into savagery, and order is restored only at the end of the novel by the entrance of an adult authority presence.

2. The Rousseauian lens. Named after the French philosopher Jean-Jacques Rousseau, the Rousseauian lens perceives children and childhood very differently. The child is seen as an embodiment of primordial innocence—Adam before the Fall—a wellspring of natural moral order. Rousseau perceived the innocence of childhood as being systematically corrupted by the pernicious influences of a competitive, cruel, and controlling society. He perceived this corruption taking place in the traditional schooling of his age. He believed that evil was not a naturally occurring phenomenon but rather a learned state. In *Emile*, Rousseau's (1762/1993) treatise on education, learning (as opposed to schooling) is presented as a natural and gentle process that taps into the child's preexisting curiosity, creativity, and motivation.

In literature, perhaps the most passionate expression of this romantic view of childhood is captured in the poetry of William Wordsworth. The child is perceived to embody a natural wisdom and is described as "father to the man" ("My Heart Leaps Up," 1802, line 7). There is also an almost divine quality to childhood and the child is described as "trailing clouds of glory" ("Ode: Intimations of Immortality From Recollections of Early Childhood," 1807, line 65).

One of the most controversial examples of a Rousseauian perception of childhood was a school founded originally in Germany but later moved to Great Britain. Developed by A. S. Neill (1992), Summerhill School was a truly radical experiment in which there were no adult-determined rules, punishments, or negative consequences for antisocial or disruptive behavior. The organization of the school, the schedule of classes, and the actual curricula were determined by the students themselves. Like Rousseau, Neill believed that children were inherently good and that if provided with freedom they would naturally gravitate toward responsible and constructive behavior. The difficulty with any enclave community, such as Summerhill, that derives its identity and raison d'etre from attacking a corrupt and cruel external society is that its graduates had an extremely difficult time reintegrating into the society they had come to despise.

3. The Confucian lens. As globalization is increasingly a reality, it is very useful for Western teachers to understand something of the Confucian worldview and this particular lens into childhood. While the word *Confucian* has an historical link to China and the Far East, many of the attributes of the Confucian perception of childhood can be found in traditional and immigrant societies around the world.

Confucian values include an emphasis on the collective welfare of the group as opposed to our more Western focus on individual autonomy. Confucian collectivism is seen in the subjugation of individual needs and desires to the furtherance of the larger group. This might be manifest in profound loyalty to one's family, one's village or tribe, one's employer, or even as an expression of nationalistic patriotism. Confucian societies are hierarchical, with the elders occupying a revered position. Ancestors and the accomplishments of past generations are greatly honored, and stability and social cohesiveness are highly valued. Children are expected to honor and respect their parents and teachers. One of the greatest compliments that the young can pay to a highly skilled elder artisan is to imitate the master. This focus on imitative learning can often lead to confused perceptions of plagiarism in young Asian students who attend Western-oriented schools.

In Confucian cultures, learning is perceived to be the transfer of the knowledge and values of the previous generation to the younger generation so that the collective good and stability of the society is preserved.

Children are not expected to challenge ideas or think critically or independently. Such thought might prove disruptive to the common order.

In Confucian and other traditional societies, Western syllogistic thinking (if $a = b$ and $c = a$, then $c = b$) is often replaced with an Eastern search for a middle way. Nisbett (2003) suggests that it is no accident that algebra developed in ancient Greece and geometry in China. He theorizes that thousands of years of cultural values and behaviors have actually affected the way in which Eastern and Western students think. Western either-or thinking lends itself to the intellectual development of disciplines such as algebra, the experimental sciences, and precedent-based jurisprudence. On the other hand, Eastern thinking tends to be more expansive (as opposed to reductionist), more inclusive of both the foreground and the background, and more focused on social cohesion and stability.

Respect for teachers on the part of a child brought up in a Confucian or traditional culture can be manifested by what may appear to be quiet passivity. This often provides Western teachers with a challenge, particularly in the area of English as a second language where active engagement with the content is perceived to be a key to learning.

A sign in a Buddhist temple in Japan reads, "Speak only if you can improve on the silence."

4. The Malthusian lens. Thomas Malthus was the nineteenth-century British economist who postulated that the supply of food increases arithmetically, whereas the population grows geometrically. Through the Malthusian lens, children are perceived as either economic assets or liabilities. We see children viewed as economic assets in developing economies that are reliant on agriculture. In subsistence-farming communities, children are frequently viewed as critically important workers upon which the actual survival of the family may depend. Birthrates often reflect this perception. This is also borne out in the recent negative population growth rates in some affluent Western countries where children may increasingly be perceived as economic liabilities.

We even see the legacy of the Malthusian lens in Western societies where our school calendar still contains a long summer vacation because a century or so ago the children were needed to work in the fields. In fact, much of the twentieth-century "industrialized" model of American education (the influence of Frederick Winslow Taylor, 2007, and *The Principles of Scientific Management*) can be interpreted through a Malthusian lens. In a century ushered in by Henry Ford's assembly lines, it was understood that most children would grow up to work in repetitive and mindless jobs in factories. What better training than the repetitive and boring rote learning of the mid-twentieth-century schoolhouse!

The Malthusian perception of childhood manifests itself regularly in our schools when we hear parents and board members talk about how students need to be prepared for the "real world of work" or when educational success is reduced to acceptance at a prestigious university.

5. *The Deweyan lens.* At about the same time as Henry Ford and others were industrializing America, John Dewey was at Columbia and the University of Chicago rethinking the nineteenth-century perception of children and childhood. He radically challenged a number of cherished beliefs. First of all, he challenged the notion that childhood was somehow a "preparation for life." Dewey believed that childhood was not preparation for anything but was an essential part of life. When childhood is perceived as preparation, it is construed as a means to an end, and it is seen as having little, if any, intrinsic value. It is a stage that one needs to grow out of as soon as possible. A natural consequence of this perception is that childhood is not respected and the period of time a child spends in school becomes a "quarantine" of sorts.

Dewey (2001) also challenged the prevailing notion that children were simply empty vessels that teachers would fill with facts and knowledge. He understood that for children (and adults) learning is fostered in active engagement with the concepts to be learned. Children need to work with ideas, to explore concepts, and to apply them. It was Dewey and others in the Progressive Movement in education who set the stage for constructivism, active engagement, cooperative learning, and many of the other elements that we frequently see in schools today. It was also Dewey who, like Jefferson before him, saw the critical link between high-quality, universal education and the maintenance of democracy and freedom.

We readily concede that these lenses are generalizations and that there are numerous other ways in which children and childhood can be perceived. We recognize that while these perceptions have positive values embedded within them, they can be subject to abuse—particularly when one lens is embraced at the expense of the others. Accordingly, we believe that as teachers it is important to "uncover" our own perceptions of childhood, Bruner's (1996) so-called folk pedagogies, as they will almost certainly color and shape the way in which we manage classrooms and plan learning for our students.

In the next chapter, we will continue our examination of how teachers come to know themselves. Specifically, we will examine how perceptions influence teacher expectations and how powerful those expectations can be in terms of student achievement. We will also consider how teachers influence what students attribute their respective success and failure to and how this affects future learning.

Activities, Exercises, and Case Studies for Self-Awareness

INFORMATIONAL AND TRANSFORMATIONAL LEARNING

Too often, teacher professional development is limited to informational learning—a focus on acquiring new knowledge and skills. The implication is that enhanced knowledge and skills will automatically result in improved classroom instruction and, therefore, improved student learning. What this assumption does not take into account is the dismal rate of transfer of theory, skills, and knowledge from the professional development workshop to classroom practice (Joyce & Showers, 2002). Informational learning only influences classroom practice when it occurs in a transformational context.

Transformational teacher learning connects theory, knowledge, and skills to our deeply held beliefs and values about education. Transformational learning helps us to explore and develop our professional identities. Robert Dilts (1994) has proposed a theory of "nested learning" (see Figure 2.1). He suggests that there is an interrelated hierarchy of adult learning. Each level of the hierarchy is contained or "nested" in the level above it. So for example, values and beliefs form a part of identity. Dilts suggests that when we focus teaching at the highest levels of the hierarchy, we can provide for a transformational learning experience.

Garmston (2005) writes that if we wish to create a learning experience that will affect one level, we need to focus our instruction on the levels above it.

Transformational teaching takes place at the intersection where procedural knowledge meets declarative knowledge, and together, this knowledge resonates with our personal values and speaks to the person we believe we are coming to be.

In the design of the activities that follow, we have attempted to embed a transformational learning context.

CARD STACK AND SHUFFLE

Our assumptions exert an enormously powerful influence on our behavior and decision making. More often than not, our assumptions are held at an unexamined or even subconscious level. For example, we might ask how our assumptions about intelligence affect our instructional behavior.

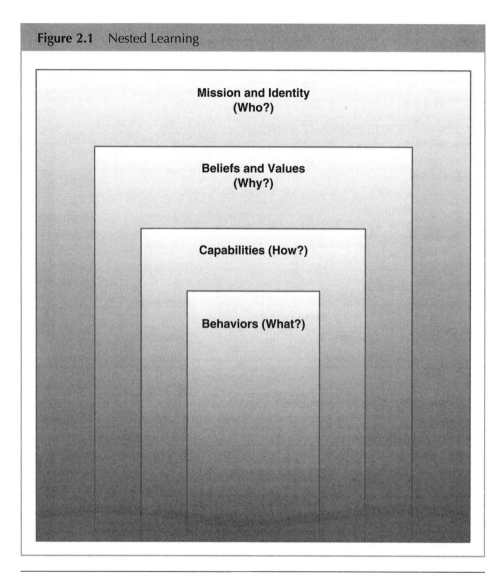

Figure 2.1   Nested Learning

Mission and Identity
(Who?)

Beliefs and Values
(Why?)

Capabilities (How?)

Behaviors (What?)

Source: Dilts, (1994).

To what degree do we believe that intelligence is monolithic (as in a single IQ score)? Or to what degree do we believe that intelligence is multifaceted and malleable (that it can be developed over time)? These assumptions can exert a powerful influence over our decision making and behavior.

One activity that we have used to support teachers in their "uncovering" of assumptions is the Card Stack and Shuffle. The activity works like this:

1. Form participants into table groups of five or six.

2. Distribute two 3 × 5 inch index cards to each participant.

3. Ask the participants to individually and without consultation complete two sentence stems, one on each card. The cards are written anonymously. The sentence stems should be genuinely open-ended but linked to key ideas or values. For example, in a workshop on teacher leadership, the sentence stems might be

    o "The very best school leaders . . ."
    o "What concerns me most about my leadership is . . ."

4. Once the individuals have completed their two cards, these cards are collected by one member of the table group and given a thorough shuffle.

5. The cards are then passed to a different table group so that no table group is analyzing its own assumptions.

6. One member of each table group turns a card over and reads it aloud. The table group then explores what assumptions are embedded in the sentence and what implications there might be. It is often helpful to have a recorder in each table group make a T-chart and record the assumptions that have been identified and their implications.

LEARNING STYLE INVENTORY

Directions: In each of the twelve rows, tick off one or two descriptions (Visual, Auditory, or Kinesthetic) that best represent your view of yourself. Give one point for each tick, one-half point if two boxes are checked in the same row. After marking your selection in each of the twelve rows, total the number of ticks for each of the columns: Visual, Auditory, and Kinesthetic. The column with the highest point count represents your preferred learning modality.

	Visual	Auditory	Kinesthetic
Learning Style	Learns best by seeing visible representations, videos, or demonstrations	Learns best by listening to verbal instructions	Learns best through movement, doing something, active engagement
Reading	Exhibits intense concentration, often pauses in reading to imagine a scene or to contemplate connections	Enjoys theater, stage plays, and dialogue; doesn't care for lengthy descriptive passages; illustrations can get in the way of meaning	May fidget when reading, may not be an enthusiastic reader, likes action stories

	Visual	Auditory	Kinesthetic
Spelling	Recognizes words by sight, relies on configuration of words, often cannot "sound out" words	Uses a phonetic approach, is able to "sound out" words	Writes words in order to sense whether they "feel" right, may be a poor speller
Handwriting	Tends to write neatly and legibly, appearance is important, spacing and size are appropriate	May write faintly and say strokes when forming letters, may have difficulty with handwriting as a young child	May push harder on pencil or pen, handwriting may deteriorate when space on the page becomes limited
Memory	Remembers visual images such as faces, writes things down, makes a list of things to do	Remembers names but not faces, remembers things by saying them aloud	Remembers best what was actually engaged in, not what was seen or spoken about
Imagery	Thinks in pictures, colors, and textures; has a rich imagination	May talk to oneself, subvocalizes, details are not important	Though images are not important, images that do occur are often associated with movement
Distractibility	Generally unaware of sound, but can be distracted by visual overload or movement	Easily distracted by sound: background noise or music	Generally inattentive to visual or auditory presentations: may appear distracted
Problem Solving	Organizes thoughts in writing, careful and linear, makes a list	Talks through a problem, will try out solutions verbally, may talk to self	Leaps into problem solving, may be impulsive, often selects the solution that involves the greatest activity
Response to Inactivity	Stares, doodles	Talks to neighbors, talks to self, hums	Fidgets, taps pencil on desk, finds reasons to move: drink of water, toilet, visit to nurse

(Continued)

(Continued)

	Visual	Auditory	Kinesthetic
Emotional Response	Exhibits distinct facial expressions; relatively easy to read; will cry when upset, stare when angry, beam when happy	Expresses emotions verbally, will change pitch and tone of voice to express emotion, will shout with joy or anger	Body reaction is an accurate barometer of emotion; will jump for joy, hug, or stamp off when angry
Appreciation of Arts	Prefers the visual arts, may not view music as holding great significance	Favors music; enjoys talking about visual arts, but may miss significant details	Responds to music through movement; may dance almost involuntarily; likes arts that can be touched, e.g., sculpture
Communication	Generally quiet, probably won't talk at length, favors visual metaphors such as "I see what you mean."	Will enjoy listening, but can't wait to talk; will use auditory metaphors such as "That really resonates with me."	Generally doesn't listen well, uses gestures when speaking, uses sports or motion metaphors such as "I'm batting a thousand."
Total Points in Each Column			

Source: From *Cognitive Coaching Foundation Seminar Learning Guide,* 7th ed., by Arthur Costa and Robert Garmston. Revised by Jane Ellison and Carolee Hays, 2007, pp. 70–71, Highlands Ranch, CO: Center for Cognitive Coaching.

QUESTIONS ABOUT LEARNING STYLE THAT TEACHERS MIGHT WANT TO ASK THEMSELVES

What Pattern or Patterns Are Emerging?

Do I concentrate better when listening to music?	
Do I doodle in meetings or while on the phone?	
Have I identified some subjects (math, foreign languages, music, etc.) that I'm just not good at?	
Am I able to remember the lyrics of a song?	

Do I prefer a map to oral directions? How easily do I read maps?	
Do I need something to fidget with when I'm concentrating?	
Do I picture something in my head when I'm trying to memorize it?	
Do I do my best work in the morning, afternoon, or evening?	
Do I learn best by doing something practical?	
Do I become frustrated when I don't understand "the big picture"?	
Do I prefer to learn in a group or by myself?	

PERCEPTIONS OF CHILDHOOD INVENTORY

Directions: Rank the statements below in the order that you prefer them from 1 through 5, with 1 being the most preferable and 5 being the least preferable.

1. The purpose of education

    A ____ is to develop student self-directedness in learning.

    B ____ is to prepare the young adult for the real world of work.

    C ____ is to help students to understand the relationships that bind us together.

    D ____ is for students to discover their talents, strengths, and creativity in an environment devoid of coercion.

    E ____ is to prepare the next generation for responsible citizenship.

2. The most effective curriculum

    A ____ is relevant to the child and taps into his or her natural curiosity.

    B ____ teaches respect, compassion, and self-sacrifice.

    C ____ sets a young person on the road to success in life.

    D ____ engages students in active learning so that they construct personal meaning.

    E ____ focuses on the great thinkers of the past so that students learn the wisdom of history.

3. A well-educated child

    A ____ makes healthy and constructive decisions because he or she has had the freedom to explore and discover responsibility.

B ___ is an independent, critical, and creative thinker.

C ___ is a self-controlled, contributing member of society.

D ___ will gain admission to a good university.

E ___ promotes the stability and welfare of the group by respectful behavior and compromise.

4. The most effective teacher

A ___ supports and facilitates children as they explore ideas and concepts and apply them.

B ___ teaches collaboration, values team work and collective effort.

C ___ is skillful at class management and has a broad repertoire of strategies.

D ___ produces the highest standardized test scores.

E ___ provides an environment of care and compassion that allows children to explore and nurtures curiosity.

5. Preferred sayings

A ___ Individual self-expression must never be at the expense of the greater good.

B ___ It is no accident that there is a relationship between education and success in life. People with lower incomes, on the whole, have a lower level of education than people with higher incomes.

C ___ Children will not understand right and wrong unless they are explicitly taught.

D ___ Power corrupts, and absolute power (especially in the classroom) corrupts absolutely.

E ___ Education supports the preservation of democracy.

In the grid below, fill in the numbers in each row that correspond to each letter For example, for Statement 1, if you ranked A as 3rd, then fill in a 3 next to A (listed below *Deweyan* for Statement 1); if you ranked B as 2nd, then fill in a 2 next to B (listed below *Malthusian* for this statement), and so on. Then, total each column to identify the respective perceptions of childhood that link most closely to your responses. In this case, the lowest total reflects the strongest association. You may wish to examine patterns in your responses and reflect on how these connect with your deeply held values.

Statement Number	Hobbesian	Rousseauian	Malthusian	Confucian	Deweyan
1	E =	D =	B =	C =	A =
2	E =	A =	C =	B =	D =
3	C =	A =	D =	E =	B =
4	C =	E =	D =	B =	A =
5	C =	D =	B =	A =	E =
Totals					

CASE STUDY

Directions: Read the case study below and address the discussion questions at the end.

"The Silence of the Lambs"

"I think I'm just feeling overwhelmed," Sarah Murray responded to Harrison Cooligan's question. The fifth-grade team had been meeting for about twenty minutes and Sarah hadn't joined in the discussion. This was entirely out of character for Sarah.

"I got two more new students today." Tears were welling up in Sarah's eyes.

"Wow," Bruce Dorado spoke softly. "That's hard. You must be feeling pretty frustrated."

"Actually it isn't frustration so much as it is . . . ," Sarah paused to think about what exactly she was feeling. "I suppose I'm wondering if I'm really adequate for the job."

"Of course you're adequate," Bruce cut in quickly. "You're one of the best teachers in the elementary school."

"Hold on a second Bruce, I think you cut Sarah off," Harrison Cooligan suggested. "Sarah, what is it specifically that you're wondering about?"

"I just don't see how I can meet the needs of all the students. My class is up to twenty-four students and a full third are ESL kids. I'm all for inclusion, in theory, but in practice, it can be overwhelming."

"I know how you feel," Bruce added.

"Sarah," Harrison spoke slowly and seriously, commanding all of her attention. "Please tell me what your class would look like if you were meeting the educational needs of all your students."

Sarah didn't respond immediately, but both Harrison and Bruce respected her thought process and remained silent.

"That's a hard question. What will my class look like when I'm meeting the educational needs of all my students?" Sarah repeated the question and held her index finger to her forehead. "I guess I'd like to see all the kids on task with their assignments. And for the most part they are. We've got really good kids." Sarah used a handkerchief to dab the moist corners of her eyes. "I've been giving the ESL kids modified assignments. I'm not sure it's the right thing to do, but I didn't think they would be able to cope . . . ," Sarah stopped midsentence. Again Bruce and Harrison respected her silence.

"You know what is really difficult," Sarah announced slowly. "It's when the new ESL kids don't say anything. I don't have any idea how much they understand. I don't have any idea if I'm actually teaching them anything. Sometimes I think we're just there wasting each other's time."

"You're worried about wasting valuable learning time," Harrison said.

"I am. I don't know if they're learning anything."

"You're not sure what the silence of the new ESL students means, and it worries you," Harrison added.

"It does worry me. I'm not a trained ESL teacher."

Harrison continued, "If you were to put yourself in the place of a new ESL student, what would be your hunch about their silence?"

"I guess I'd be quiet too. I mean I know that receptive language has to develop before expressive language. Maybe there are some other ways for them to show me that they have understood a lesson."

"What have you in mind?" Harrison asked.

"Maybe I could use more nonverbal activities with them. Maybe I could develop some visual cues or symbols."

"A simple sign language?" Harrison queried.

"Exactly. Maybe I could take the ESL kids as a group for a short meeting and we could develop a secret sign language so that they could let me know when they don't understand without any embarrassment."

"I'd be happy to take your non-ESL kids while you have the meeting," Bruce volunteered.

"I suspect the ESL kids would really appreciate your concern for them," Harrison added, noting Sarah's eyes were now dry and rather bright.

Discussion Questions

1. What specific evidence do you have in the case study that Sarah is a relatively self-aware teacher?

2. What strategies do Bruce and Harrison use to support Sarah? Which are more effective?

3. What emotionally intelligent behavior is present in the case study?

3 Continuing the Journey Into Self

Perceptions, Expectations, and Attributions

This chapter continues our journey of teacher self-discovery. We will examine the powerful influence that teacher perceptions and expectations have on student learning. We will suggest that emotionally intelligent teachers constantly question their perceptions, asking themselves, "Is there another way to look at this student or that situation?" We also explore how teachers influence what children believe about their successes or failures and how these attributions can affect future learning.

PERCEPTIONS: HOW WE DEFINE MOST EVERYTHING

The old parable about heaven and hell speaks volumes about the power of perceptions. The question is asked: "What is the difference between heaven and hell?" Heaven, we are told, consists of spending all of eternity reading holy books. By way of contrast, hell consists of spending all of eternity reading holy books.

Perceptions define most everything.

As teachers, our perceptions have power and influence that extend far beyond ourselves. These perceptions are often based on assumptions that we hold at a subconscious level but nevertheless have great influence over our behavior. Take, for example, the assumption that intelligence is genetically "fixed" at birth—some kids are born bright and some are not. From this assumption may come the perception that students may arrive in our classes with specific talents, abilities, and deficits over which we, the teachers, can exert only small influence. This may salve our conscience when a child fails to meet the grade-level benchmarks, but it also may dissuade teachers from truly deciding to teach *all* children.

Our perceptions are not only the sense we make out of the world but also the process through which we actually sculpt ourselves. The holy books in heaven and hell are exactly the same. It is not the external reality that matters but rather the meaning we make of it.

Our perceptions have to do with the brain recognizing patterns. In recognizing patterns our brains form neural pathways. The more often the recognition, the stronger the pathway becomes. This is both a strength and weakness in terms of our perceptions. It is a strength in the sense that useful neural pathways become stronger. However, our selective attention seeks to confirm what we already know or think we know. Kelley (1967) suggests that we are "naïve scientists" in that when we seek to justify a perception, we generally look for only one piece of confirming evidence. For example, if we suspect a student is not exerting a great deal of effort in class and that student fails to hand in a homework assignment, our perception of "laziness" may be confirmed. Kelley recommends that we look for at least *three pieces of evidence* (data points) before framing a tentative conclusion.

Another example of how we may "fall into" unexamined perceptions can come to light when we think of some of the less-than-rational behavior of adolescents. The teenage years can be very challenging for even the most empathetic and patient teacher, and it is all too tempting to label our impulsive teenage friends as selfish, unruly, irresponsible, or lacking in judgment. However, research on the development of the brain during adolescence paints a more complex picture. Adolescents are (by virtue of their enormous hormonal changes, ongoing brain development, and neural pruning) subject to being emotionally volatile, unpredictable, self-absorbed, and hypersensitive. Willis (2007) writes that the "last parts of the brain to fully develop during the teen years are the frontal lobes—the centers of emotional stability as well as executive function, concentration, value and moral judgment, planning, and consequence prediction" (p. 76). This developmental phase lends itself to many opportunities for teacher misinterpretation. What may appear, at first glance, as teenage willfulness or defiance or recalcitrance may actually be the physiological inability of the immature brain to deal with and interpret the enormous mass of sensory stimuli that is constantly bombarding it.

By consciously suspending judgment, we promote flexibility of thought—the ability and willingness to adopt and experiment with other perspectives. We can ask, "Is there another way to look at this?" For example, if we become aware that Shamir isn't paying attention in class, we can conclude that he lacks motivation or that the content is too complex for his readiness level. With flexibility of thought we can also entertain the idea that his shortened attention span may be the brain's way of shutting out "anxiety producing confusion about material that is not being presented in an engaging and comprehensible manner" (Willis, 2007, p. 44).

TEACHER EXPECTATIONS: THE BREAKFAST OF BOTH CHAMPIONS AND LOSERS

There is also evidence from research that our expectations affect our perceptions (Goldfried & Robins, 1983; Swann & Read, 1981) and that our beliefs actually influence the types of information that we attend to and remember. "We tend to process carefully information that is consistent with our beliefs and to ignore information that suggests we are wrong" (Julian & Miller, 1984, as cited in Hatfield, Cacioppo, & Rapson, 1993, p. 96).

We also tend to confuse our perceptions with reality. Because we perceive it, we assume it exists in the form that we have constructed. For example, many of us have been made uncomfortable by overheard conversations in the faculty lounge in which children are described as "thick as two boards, lazy, clueless, or unable to chew gum and walk at the same time." Our discomfort with these derogatory remarks suggests that we sense a difference between the perception and the reality.

Many years ago, a high school principal asked a teacher to rewrite a report card that in the original included the sentence, "Roger would achieve much more in my class if he wasn't so unpleasant." The teacher came to see the principal, puzzled by his insistence that the report be rewritten. "But it's true, Roger is unpleasant," he argued. The principal then asked, "Does Roger know that you think he is unpleasant?" The teacher replied, "I believe in honesty. I told him that he needed a personality makeover."

It is hoped that Roger was able to discount the teacher's comments. However, such comments illustrate the teacher's inability to grasp the difference between Roger's uncooperative behavior and his own emotionally charged perception. In addition, such perceptions serve to illustrate how expectancy on the part of the teacher can produce a counterproductive self-fulfilling prophecy. Kids will often behave in exactly the way we expect them to—on occasion, much to our dismay.

EXPECTANCY THEORY:
PYGMALION ON HER FIRST DATE

Social psychologists have studied in detail the effects of expectations on behavior. In a classic study at the University of Minnesota (Snyder, Tanke, & Berscheid, 1977), men and women were invited to participate in what they were told was a study on the process of how couples become acquainted. Male and female subjects were directed to different rooms so that they would not meet and told that they would have their first interaction by telephone. Before the conversation began, the male subject was given a photograph of the woman he would be speaking with and a brief paragraph of bio data. In reality, the photographs were not of the woman the man would soon be speaking with. They were of either a very attractive woman or a homely one. Men who assumed that they were paired with an attractive woman *expected* her to be socially skillful—poised, gracious, and humorous. Those men who believed they were paired with less attractive women *expected* them to be socially awkward, lacking in refinement, and graciousness. Such outcomes should not surprise us. Social psychologists have long suggested that good-looking people make more positive first impressions than less attractive ones.

What surprised the researchers was that the men's *expectations* had a dramatic effect on the women's behavior. Obviously, the women who were spoken to had a wide range of physical appearances. However, in the short duration of the phone call, the women became what the men expected them to be. The women who were addressed as "beauties" were judged to be far more animated, confident, and socially adept than those who were assumed to be less attractive who, in turn, were judged to be withdrawn, lacking in confidence, and awkward. The male expectations became reflected in the women's behavior.

If such a profound effect could be achieved in a mere ten-minute telephone conversation, the effects of teacher expectations on students over the course of an entire year can be truly dramatic.

EXPECTANCY THEORY:
PYGMALION IN THE CLASSROOM

Probably the most well-known study of teacher expectations and their effect on students is the landmark *Pygmalion in the Classroom* (1992), in which Harvard researchers Robert Rosenthal and Lenore Jacobson told teachers in a San Francisco elementary school that the students they were about to inherit for the new school year were high-achieving "bloomers" and that they could expect these children to make strong achievement gains during the school year. In fact, the students had been selected at random without any formal testing or identification. However, as the year passed, these students did make significant achievements. These so-called bloomers outperformed their peers. Rosenthal and Jacobson attributed the accelerated progress of these students to teacher expectations and their differential treatment as the supposedly "gifted" students. The outcome of the research became common parlance in the educational community as "the self-fulfilling prophecy" or the "Pygmalion effect." Essentially the research study, confirmed by later research (Brophy, 1983; Cooper & Tom, 1984; Good, 1987), suggests a strong correlation between what teachers expect from or believe about students and how students actually perform. In other words, how a student performs in school is influenced heavily, some might argue actually determined, by what teachers believe and think that student is capable of.

Our expectations of students (1) are constructed by ourselves either consciously or subconsciously; (2) are often developed in comparison to other students; (3) can be profoundly influenced by colleagues (negatively and positively); and (4) most important, are malleable and subject to revision. Ramachandran and Blakeslee (1998) write that "all our perceptions—indeed, maybe all aspects of our minds—are governed by comparisons and not by absolute values. This appears to be true whether you are talking about something as obvious as judging the brightness of print in newspaper or something as subtle as detecting a blip in your internal emotional landscape" (p. 167).

Goleman (1995) discusses a study similar to the Pygmalion research undertaken in the U.S. Navy. For decades, the Navy had identified a small percentage of recruits as "unmotivated problem sailors." They used the acronym LP (low performer) to label this group of shipmates who didn't perform well at their jobs, were disruptive to communal discipline, were apathetic or rebellious, and were constantly in trouble. However, the supervisors of the so-called LPs were given a new strategy with which to deal with this recalcitrant group. They were taught to treat the LPs more like winners. In a myriad of ways, the supervisors let the LPs know that they believed in their ability to change, to become more constructive and productive seamen. Interestingly, the LPs started to perform at a higher level. They received fewer punishments, showed better all-around performances, and some even improved their personal appearance—exhibiting new pride in themselves and their work. The Pygmalion effect was at work in the U.S. Navy. Constructing positive presuppositions about others, particularly those who might otherwise attract negative perceptions, can create a powerful self-fulfilling prophecy:

> You see . . . the difference between a lady and a flower girl is how she is treated. I shall always be a flower girl to Professor Higgins, because he always treats me as a flower girl, and always will; but I know I can be a lady to you, because you always treat me as a lady, and always will.
>
> Eliza Doolittle in *Pygmalion* (Shaw, 1913, 5.137–140)

Over the past three decades, we have come to accept that positive teacher expectations are a key variable that distinguishes teachers who produce good achievement gains from those who do not (Campbell & Campbell, 1999). Having said that, it is important to add that a discussion of how those expectations are constructed, examined, and managed has received scant attention in professional circles.

Campbell & Campbell (1999) sum up this dilemma succinctly:

> To make sense of student learning potential they encounter daily, teachers construct beliefs or scripts about the intelligence of those in their charge. These implicit beliefs can be optimistic or pessimistic, constrictive or expansive. For the most part, they are seldom verbalized, usually unconscious, and may work against students' welfare. For example, if a teacher believes that intelligence cannot be modified, then schooling can accomplish little. Without educational intervention that might dislodge incorrect scripts about intelligence, or affirm and make conscious useful ones, teachers' implicit beliefs remain intact. (p. 4)

We agree that professional development intervention that supports teacher reflection on assumptions and beliefs and their implications is critically important. Teachers are not immune to misconceptions, and it is only by confronting the ones that get in the way of student learning that change will occur:

> This means encouraging prospective teachers and practicing teachers to reflect deeply on their beliefs and attitudes so that a shift can take place. . . . Teachers need to give sustained attention to these questions, and this implies that schools need to provide them with the resources and support they need for doing this kind of difficult, but in the long run, empowering work. (Nieto, 2005, p. 217)

In the hundreds of interactions that we have daily, it is easy for well-intentioned comments to be damaging to students. Elaine (Cushman, 2003) is a high school ESL student, and she writes about when her science teacher gave her a test and informed her that he didn't believe she would be able to take it because of her lack of English. The teacher went on to say that he would give Elaine a B anyway if she came to class everyday. Elaine burst into tears. The teacher's attempt at kindness undermined her self-confidence and sense of efficacy.

In this brief vignette, we see how a teacher's presumably good intentions were interpreted by the student to reflect her lack of ability. And this brings us to the knotty but important issue of how teachers influence the attribution of student success and failure.

THE FOUR HORSEMEN OF ATTRIBUTION

In 1987, Madeline Hunter and George Barker published a landmark article in which they applied attribution theory from the field of psychology (Heider, 1958; Kelley, 1967) to education. In essence, Hunter and Barker were exploring what factors children attributed their respective success or failure in school to and what effect these attributions might have on future learning. This perceived causation has been found to be extremely influential in terms of our self-esteem and our expectations of success and failure in subsequent similar learning situations.

We tend to attribute success and failure to four horsemen: inherent intelligence, personal effort, task difficulty, and luck. Most people in the West consider inherent intelligence and personal effort to be the most powerful factors in influencing success or failure. Historically, we have come to believe that the ethic of hard work and the competitive spirit of capitalism reward bright, intelligent individuals who exert considerable personal effort and rise to the challenge of competition. In other cultures, luck, fatalism, or collective identity can play a powerful role.

When we examine attribution theory in the classroom, we find three important characteristics of the perceived causes of student success or failure: locus, stability, and control (Hunter & Barker, 1987).

1. Locus. By locus we mean the location of the cause, where the responsibility for the success or failure resides: either internal to self or external to self. Internal causes include natural talents, inherent intelligence, and personal effort; whereas external causes include task difficulty and luck.

It stands to reason that if I believe my efforts will have little impact on the outcome of a project or assignment, my perception of my ability is lowered. If I didn't believe I could achieve other than an F, the failure becomes a self-fulfilling prophecy. Similarly, if my A is seen as a result of an easy assignment or teacher compassion, my self-esteem is also lowered. Pride results from accomplishment only when we attribute the achievement to an internal locus such as ability or effort.

Internal attribution of success can build learning efficacy. Albert reports that he did well on his International Baccalaureate extended essay because he has mastered time management. Naomi reports that the improvement in her writing is connected to learning how to frame a thesis statement. In each case, the outcome of their experience is attributed to controllable factors within the student.

As Madeline Hunter and George Barker (1987) explain, how the teacher responds to success or failure can have a profound influence on the student's causal attribution:

> The way a teacher responds to a student's success or failure can signal the teacher's beliefs as to whether the student is in control of success or failure. . . . For example, annoyance can say to a student that he had the ability to perform successfully and was responsible for the less-than-satisfactory performance. Sympathy and understanding can communicate that no matter how much effort a student expended, he could not have accomplished the task. For a teacher to accept less from a student than she is capable of doing can convince the student of your belief that, even with effort, she doesn't have the ability to meet expectations. Criticism of performance when the student could have done better communicates "you have the ability." (p. 53)

External attribution connects success or failure to factors and forces outside of students. Mary reports that she did well on the science project because the teacher is an "easy marker." Sanjeev states that he was "unlucky" on the questions that appeared on the quiz. Athletes will often attribute success internally, to training, hard work, or skill; and failure externally, to "bad luck" or "an unfair umpire."

2. Stability. Stability is the degree to which we perceive the cause of our success or failure to be reliably constant or subject to change. Unstable causes include personal effort and luck. Stable causes include inherent intelligence, natural talent, and task difficulty.

The relative stability of what we believe causes our success or failure is a prime ingredient in our expectations for the future. If the cause of our failure is unstable (or a lack of personal effort) it may not have a predetermined effect on future expectations. If, however, we come to attribute failure to a stable cause ("Physics is just too difficult!"), we may come to predict future failure.

There are situations in which stable causes help frame realistic limits to our aspirations. For example, someone who is tone deaf may not want to expend great effort to become an opera singer.

The danger here is the inaccurate and invalid attribution of failure to inherent intelligence or native ability. "We are a math phobic nation," Hunter and Barker (1987) write, "not because of native ability, but because of mechanically manipulating numbers with little or no meaning. . . . When students attribute success or failure to stable causes, they expect the same from the future as from the past. When they attribute success or failure to unstable causes, their expectations can change" (p. 52).

3. Control. The degree to which the cause of our success or failure is perceived to be controllable is related to individuals' sense of efficacy, the influence they believe they have in shaping future events—their potency and optimism. Personal effort is a controllable attribute; whereas talent, intelligence, task difficulty, and luck are most often perceived as beyond the power of the individual to exert much influence over.

Personal effort is perceived to be the attribution over which the individual has the most control. As a result, students tend to operate on an if-then system. *If* they perceive that the outcome can be influenced by effort, *then* they are more likely to work hard. If, on the other hand, students create the perception that they are no good at learning a second language, mathematics, music, or so forth, it is highly unlikely that they will expend great effort in that arena.

Research on peak performers in a multitude of different fields (Csikszentmihalyi, 1991) shows that the key variable in highly successful people is hard work and consistent effort. The implication for students is clear; if they are to maximize their opportunities for success, they must come to perceive a positive, influential relationship between effort and achievement.

TO BE YOUNG, GIFTED, AND FRAGILE

Much of the learning fragility of highly gifted students derives from an attribution of their success in school to their inherent intelligence, something they have little control or influence over. Teachers and parents inadvertently feed this perception by attempting to motivate students by telling them how bright or clever they are. These naturally talented students often do extremely well in school until they encounter a minor failure (e.g., a problem that is too complex to solve in the head). Then they tend not to exhibit resilience. They tend not to "fail forward." Their lack of resilience can be seen as a natural product of believing their previous success was caused by factors (high native intelligence) outside their control or influence.

When children connect their successful learning to factors residing within themselves that are predictable and that they can directly influence, these children develop the optimal conditions necessary for resilience and future learning. They are developing learning efficacy, flexibility, and most important, optimism. When they do fail, they are able to fail forward, learn from their mistakes and enter a new learning experience energized. Van Overwalle and De Metsenaere (1990) found that students who make the correlation between effort and achievement attained their goals more readily than did students who were simply taught techniques for time management and comprehension of new material.

LEARNED HELPLESSNESS IN THE CLASSROOM

There are some disturbing connections between attribution theory and stress-response theory. While moderate, transient stress can actually enhance learning and memory formation, long-term, chronic stress can be cognitively debilitating. Sapolsky (2004) identifies five conditions that can create or exacerbate stress: loss of personal control over the situation, loss of predictability in the occurrence of the stressor, a loss of social support, a loss of outlets for frustration, and a perception that things are getting worse. Under these circumstances, our stress responses move from mild to nightmarish.

Sapolsky (2004) cites studies of laboratory rats that were subjected to irritating electrical shocks. One group of rats had been trained that they could avoid the shock by pushing a lever. Even when the lever didn't work to stop the shocks, the rats who *believed* they had a degree of control over their environment experienced considerably less stress, developed fewer ulcers, and had stronger immune systems. In a similar series of experiments, when the electrical shocks became unpredictable, the stress levels of the rats increased, even when the actual number of shocks per time interval decreased.

What happens to rats that are chronically stressed and perceive the situation to be unpredictable and beyond their control? They develop what the psychologists call *learned helplessness*. While scientists often object to making connections between experiments on laboratory animals and human beings, we think it is reasonable to draw some conjectures between the learned helplessness of laboratory animals and students in our schools. If these connections are valid, the implications for teachers may be serious.

In the laboratory, the condition of learned helplessness is quite generalized. The animal has trouble coping with all sorts of varied tasks after its exposure to uncontrolled stressors:

> Such helplessness extends to tasks having to do with its ordinary life, like competing with another animal for food, or avoiding social aggression. . . . Animals suffering from learned helplessness share many psychological features with depressed humans. Such animals have a motivational problem—one of the reasons that they are helpless is that they often do not even attempt a coping response when they are in a new situation. . . . Animals with learned helplessness also have a cognitive problem, something awry with how they perceive the world and think about it. When they do make the rare coping response, they can't tell whether it works or not. (Sapolsky, 2004, p. 301)

So the first question is: Is it possible that the stresses experienced by students involved in the attribution of learning problems (attributions that are uncontrollable and unpredictable, e.g., "I'm just not good at math") result in a form of learned helplessness? Sapolsky (2004) believes they do and comments that it takes "surprisingly little in terms of uncontrollable unpleasantness to make humans give up and become helpless in a generalized way" (p. 302).

Sapolsky (2004) writes about a series of experiments with human volunteers conducted by Donald Hiroto who showed that unpleasant and uncontrollable stressors do create learned helplessness. Hiroto exposed student volunteers to loud and unpleasant noises. For one group, the noises were inescapable; for the other, they were escapable. However, the two groups were paired so that they were both exposed to the same amount of noise. Following their exposure to the noise, both groups were given a learning activity. The group that had been exposed to inescapable noise was significantly less capable of learning the task. Hiroto and Seligman (as cited in Sapolsky, 2004) conducted a follow-up experiment of a similar design. After exposure to the unpleasant noise, the two groups were given simple word puzzles to solve. Again, the group without perceived control was less able to problem solve.

In yet another study, Hiroto and Seligman (as cited in Sapolsky, 2004) asked volunteers to pick a card of a certain color according to rules that would become apparent to the subject as the activity proceeded. In the control group, the rules could be discerned. However, in the experimental group, the different color cards were at random and it was impossible for the volunteers to learn the rules. Afterward, the experimental group was much less capable of coping with a simple and easily solved task. Seligman has also shown that the debilitating effects of such learned helplessness extend into social coping situations.

So the second question is: Can the behavior of teachers induce learned helplessness in students?

LEARNING DISABLED VERSUS TEACHING DISABLED

There would seem to be certain conditions that might make a student more susceptible to learned helplessness. Perhaps the most powerful indicator is whether the young person has an internal or external locus of control. If the students have an internal locus of control, they have enhanced levels of efficacy and believe they are, to a large extent, in control of their lives. They are self-confident and see themselves as the architects of their own future. These students are much less susceptible to learned helplessness than those who attribute outcomes to luck or chance or who attribute failure to internal attributes that are uncontrollable (e.g., intelligence).

Ironically, teachers may send unintended attribution messages with the best of intentions. When Bill was in the seventh grade, he struggled with French. At the end of the year, he had earned a D for the course. The French teacher was sympathetic and told him that some people just don't have a knack for languages, and she suggested that he switch to Spanish the following year as it was "an easier language." Bill did so, and fifty odd years later remains distressingly monolingual—not withstanding the fact that he lives a good part of the year in France!

Some children are learning disabled. Other children can be teaching disabled.

LET THEM LEARN CHINESE!

Learned helplessness in the classroom can take place on an individual basis, for example, when a child comes to believe that he or she cannot learn a foreign language or doesn't have an aptitude for music. Even more disturbing is when a collective perception serves to instill learned helplessness in a group, for example, the traditional (and to some extent still prevailing) notion that girls don't have an aptitude for higher-level math or science courses. Sapolsky cites a chilling demonstration of this learned helplessness in a group of inner-city school kids with severe reading problems. Were the children intellectually incapable of reading?

Apparently not, the psychologists circumvented the students' resistance to learning to read by, instead, teaching them Chinese characters. Within hours they were capable of reading more complex symbolic sentences than they could in English. The children had apparently been previously taught all too well that reading English was beyond their ability. (Rozin, Poritsky, & Sotsky, 1971, as cited in Sapolsky, 2004, p. 304)

PERCEPTIONS OF SONYA

Attribution theory also has powerful implications for the teacher in the classroom. Are we attributing learning difficulties to factors that neither the student nor the teacher has influence over? If, for example, we attribute Sonya's lack of motivation and apathetic attitude to a dysfunctional home life, an alcoholic mother, and an absent father, we have selected attribution factors that are for the most part beyond the control or influence of either Sonya or her teachers. While there may be no denying Sonya's miserable home life, the attribution of it as a cause of Sonya's indolence is a mental construction that lives within the perceptions of the teacher and possibly also within the learned helplessness of the child.

Imagine a different perception in the case of Sonya. Despite her wretched home life, Sonya has considerable gifts and strengths, which at the moment she is not applying to schoolwork. As Sonya's teacher, I need to explore ways to support her in gaining access to her own inner resources. I need to find opportunities in the classroom for her to use her strengths and develop greater self-confidence in her learning. Sonya faces more challenges than most students. She will have greater need of those inner resources and much greater need of teacher perceptions of her that are filled with possibilities rather than dead ends.

In this later perception, the teacher has assumed an internal attribution. She has not stopped exploring Sonya's learning difficulties simply because the student comes from a dysfunctional family. The teacher is actively looking for ways to support Sonya's learning and to bolster her self-esteem.

How important is this perceptual shift in teachers? With children who will succeed anyway, probably not very. But with children who are at risk, children with learning disabilities, gifted students, youngsters who come from dysfunctional families, or students with emotional or behavioral problems, it is arguably the single most important predictor of success or failure in school. Research into resilient children (Brooks & Goldstein, 2001) illustrates clearly that, almost without exception, children who face extraordinary hardships in childhood (extreme poverty, physical or sexual abuse, alcoholic parents, etc.) and who manage to grow into successful, productive, and caring adults had at least one significant adult in their childhood (often not their parents or even a relative) whom they could trust and rely upon. That significant adult was often a teacher who refused to give up on them—a teacher who was able to construct a perception of the child based upon internal and controllable attributions.

It is our contention that to meet diverse student learning needs teachers must explore their belief systems and "mine" or deconstruct their perceptions. Unlike Roger's teacher who perceived the young man's "unpleasantness" to be an inherent characteristic of the student, we need to understand that perceptions are manufactured by the perceiver and are not simply the result of sensory input from a fixed external reality. We need to appreciate how our classroom perceptions of students and their potential are built upon *our own* belief systems, *our* cultural values, *our* previous experiences, and *our* prejudices and biases. This is unquestionably demanding and challenging work, but if we are to be responsive to individual learning needs, it must be undertaken.

Teachers need to ask themselves explicitly: "What are my perceptions of this class or that student?" "How have I constructed them?" "What are they based upon?" "Where is the data?" "What have I selected to pay attention to that has led me to that perception?" "What am I choosing not to pay attention to?"

Years ago, Ochan was a member of a child-study team at Jakarta International School that met weekly to discuss students who were encountering problems with their learning. After several such meetings, one member of the team suggested that the group had been focusing almost exclusively on children's deficits, what students were unable to do. The member suggested that more attention be given to student strengths. As a result of this suggestion, a whiteboard was installed in the team room, and before any child was discussed, the board was divided in half with labels *weaknesses* and *strengths*. By consensus, the team agreed never to leave a meeting with the strengths portion of the whiteboard empty. This is a simple example of how individuals and groups can "mine" their perceptions and gain some control over them. If we do not understand and control our perceptions, they will certainly control us.

In a Cognitive Coaching workshop in the French Pyrenees, Bob Garmston asked the teacher participants to reflect on the statement: "That student made me mad." The conversations that followed illustrated the power of examining or mining our perceptions. Participants identified that the anger being described was being produced by the teacher and was not a necessary or even a direct product of the student's behavior. One participant even asked why the teacher would relinquish such emotional control to a student. Other participants suggested that the angry response might have been a default position and that other responses could have been selected if the individual's perceptions of the event had been consciously explored. Still others suggested that pausing to suspend judgment might have led to deeper understanding. Others examined the "false causality" implied in the statement and applied it to other classroom situations. All the participants were engaged in mining how our perceptions can influence our professional response behaviors.

AM I PART OF THE PROBLEM OR PART OF THE SOLUTION?

One of the most important and least asked introspective questions that a teacher can frame is "whether my professional self-esteem is part of the problem." Teachers are no different from the general population in that we need to find satisfaction and meaning in our work. We need to feel successful. We rejoice when our students succeed; when they master a new skill, score well on an examination, or are accepted to a prestigious university. But how do we deal with the student who appears not to be succeeding? How do we rationalize to ourselves the child who, despite our best efforts, is failing our class? Too often we, like the hedgehog, roll ourselves in a fetal ball with our sharp quills pointing outward. In other words, we "write off" the failing student as being unmotivated or behaviorally challenged or as having a learning disability or ADHD (attention-deficit hyperactivity disorder) in order to protect our fragile professional self-esteem. Unfortunately many of our colleagues, in good-natured attempts to bolster our flagging efficacy, inadvertently promote the student write off. "I had Norma in my class last year, and honestly, I didn't do any better with her." "Ryan shouldn't be in this school. I don't know why the administration keeps admitting children who don't want to learn."

We need to uncover our perceptions, particularly the negative ones, about students. We should not be satisfied with an empty label or overused jargon that seems to allow us off the hook.

A number of years ago, we were in a child-study team meeting during a discussion of a very bright child whose behavior was disrupting the class. It was a tense discussion because the child's teacher was clearly feeling defensive about how Ronny's "fooling around" was disrupting the learning of other children. After the discussion had labored on for more than half an hour, the chair of the meeting announced that Ronny was obviously exhibiting "attention-seeking behavior." There was almost an audible sigh of relief from the participants. Now that Ronny had been given a label, we could move on to the next item on the agenda and away from the tension-filled issue at hand. But the classroom teacher, to her credit, wasn't ready to do so. She understood that we weren't finished with the problem-identification stage of our discussion. "That may be," she said. "But it doesn't help me tomorrow." She knew intuitively how important it is to get beneath the labels. We need to make our expectations of individual students explicit. We need to be ruthlessly honest with ourselves about our emotional reactions to different children and the assumptions that guide and even determine our response behavior.

CONCLUSION: WHEN A VICTIM BECOMES A SURVIVOR

We began this chapter with the heading "Perceptions: How We Define Most Everything." The power of perceptual shift was illustrated to us recently in a powerful way. Geetha, the wife of a teacher colleague and friend, was at home in the middle of the day. An intruder broke into the house and savagely beat her so that she had to be hospitalized and, for some time, was in danger of losing her eyesight. Her husband, Kenny, reflected on the intense emotions that both he and Geetha underwent during this period: fear, violation, bitterness, and rage. For both of them, the horrific experience was transformational. Geetha described her perceptual shift, "I stopped being a victim the moment he stopped hitting and kicking me. Now I am a survivor!" (K. Peavy, personal communication, 2009).

Much of what we perceive as the external world—whether it is the physical world or the emotional realm of relationships—is profoundly shaped and even defined by what we pay attention to. The process through which we select what to pay attention to is both conscious and subconscious. Some of it is hardwired into our brains by a hundred thousand years of survival necessity. Some of it, on the other hand, we can have control and influence over.

When we become more flexible in constructing our perceptions, we explore alternative interpretations for student behavior. We are more open to new information, connections, questions, and hypotheses. Simply gathering learning data about a specific child can change our outlook on that child.

The greater our professional self-knowledge—the more intimately we know ourselves as teachers—the greater our power to consciously select what we wish to pay attention to. The old adage is nowhere more true than in our classrooms: "The key is not to see new things, but to see old things with new eyes."

In closing this chapter, we leave you with one of Bill's favorite questions when interviewing prospective teachers: "What do your students learn from you that you don't explicitly teach?"

Activities, Exercises, and Case Studies That Promote Teacher Self-Awareness

BUILDING FLEXIBILITY OF THOUGHT: TALES OUT OF SCHOOL

Directions: For each of the vignettes below, address the questions that follow. The questions are designed to help you consider a variety of perspectives.

Nishad

Nishad's mother is waiting to see you for a parent conference. Nishad is in the fifth grade and is struggling in virtually all his subjects. His frustration threshold is low, and you have noticed an increasing number of temper outbursts. Nishad has not been formally assessed for a learning disability. Informal observation suggests he is reading on a first- or second-grade level. He steadfastly refuses to write but loves to draw pictures in art. He is constantly losing his books and papers.

Nishad's mother is a single parent. She is aggressive and domineering and blames the school for Nishad's difficulties. She has her heart set on Nishad becoming a medical doctor.

- What positive factors might be motivating Nishad's mother?
- What are some mutually positive outcomes that the conference might achieve?
- What strategies might you use to facilitate the conference?

Marina

Marina poses a problem in terms of admission and placement. Originally, Marina comes from a primitive hunter-gatherer tribe in the remote southern islands in the Philippines. Her first language was her tribal mother tongue. Following the death of her parents, Marina at age seven was moved to an orphanage in Manila where she was spoken to exclusively in Tagalog. Two years later, she was adopted by German missionaries and began to learn German.

Marina's adoptive parents have now been transferred to the United States, and they are applying for her admission to your school.

Marina is age-appropriate for the seventh grade, but there are serious questions whether she can cope with the level of work. Physically mature, Marina is socially quite shy and withdrawn.

- What perspectives need to be taken into account in this situation?
- What are some assumptions that might underlie this decision-making process?
- What might be some emotionally intelligent ways to proceed?

Matthias

Matthias is a child in the third grade who has a learning disability. He was evaluated and diagnosed some twelve months ago and since that time has been making excellent progress in your class. This has been due in large part to the partnership you have formed with Matthias's mother. You have worked closely with her, and a trusting relationship has resulted.

Matthias understands that he learns differently than other children in the class. However, he also believes that he is a capable student who can succeed in school.

The school year is coming to an end and Matthias's mother requests that he be retained in the third grade next year. You are puzzled by the request and telephone her about it. When questioned further, Matthias's mother bursts into tears and admits that her concern centers on the personality of the one fourth-grade teacher who has a reputation for no-nonsense discipline and sarcasm.

- How might you paraphrase Matthias's mother's concern?
- What deep values come into play?
- What might be an emotionally intelligent way to proceed?

Carmen

Carmen is in the ninth grade. Her last report card was mixed, but the comment of her music teacher has stayed with you: "Carmen continues to function adequately in music, but I sense there is a wealth of untapped talent—not just musical talent, intellectual talent—which we, as her teachers, are missing. I have watched Carmen take a backseat to her peers in class discussions and projects. It is almost as though if she showed herself to be gifted, this would in some way ostracize her from her friends."

Her English teacher was more prosaic: "Carmen is an above-average student who is going through all the usual ninth-grade girl-boy stuff that is the bane of the ninth grade. All this is naturally interfering with her school work."

Last year, Carmen won a prize for writing an operetta titled *Codex 1181,* a work inspired by the 1633 trial of Galileo Galilei.

Last month, Carmen's father wrote to the school complaining that his daughter was not being assigned homework.

Last week, Carmen was found smoking in the girls' toilet.

Yesterday, she cut school and was suspended by the principal.

- As her homeroom teacher, what questions might you ask Carmen that would allow you greater insight into her present situation?
- If all behavior is a result of thought, what might be some possible reasons behind Carmen's recent behavior?

Stefano

Stefano joined the school earlier this year as a student in your sixth-grade class. Before entering the school, Stefano spoke almost no English. His previous schooling was in Italian, and his reports indicate that he had been an above-average student. The transfer to the present school has been a difficult one for Stefano. He left a close circle of friends in Italy and for the first few weeks appeared insecure and reticent. In addition to his regular schooling, Stefano attends Italian language classes twice a week and on Saturday mornings goes to catechism class.

At the present time, Stefano's English is insufficient for him to deal with the abstract concepts that he will have to encounter in the seventh grade. The question you have been asked to address is whether Stefano should begin the study of a foreign language in the seventh grade. His father wants him to study French. The guidance counselor believes that an additional language will simply serve to confuse him and that Stefano should use the time for additional English.

- How might you approach this impasse in an emotionally intelligent manner?

INSIGHT MINING IN ACTION: UNMASKING SUCCESS

When teachers are working with struggling students, it is often difficult for them to perceive the progress that the students have actually made. We often become so obsessed with the child's deficits that we miss the strengths.

One activity that we have developed for use in teacher workshops draws on Suzanne Stevens's (1997) work on envisioning. We have titled it "Unmasking Success." In essence, the activity asks teachers to think about and analyze a student who is currently presenting them with a learning challenge. At the same time, it requires teachers to uncover, deconstruct, and reframe their perceptions of the student, drawing upon the student's strengths so as to envision specifically what success might look like for this student at some point in the future.

The Unmasking Success activity works as follows:

1. Participants are asked to think about a student they are currently teaching who is presenting them with a challenge of one sort or another in the classroom. Three minutes of silent recollection follow.

2. Participants are then asked to respond in writing to the following questions about the student:

- What specifically does the student struggle with?
- When have I seen this student doing his or her best work?
- What are the student's interests and strengths?
- What strategies have I tried with this student?
- What are my preconceptions and expectations of this student?
- What questions am I generating about this student's learning profile?

3. Participants are given five minutes to discuss their responses to the questions with a learning partner. The partners are asked to listen, paraphrase, and probe for clarity and specificity but to refrain from judgment or offering advice.

4. Participants are then given a sheet of poster board and an eclectic collection of magazines and are instructed to make a pictorial collage of their vision of success this student may achieve by the end of the school year. The poster may only include pictures (no words or phrases). This compels the participants into highly personalized, metaphoric thinking. The participants are further instructed to write out on the back of the poster a brief description of why each picture or photograph was selected and its specific connection to success for this specific child.

5. Once the posters are completed, each participant makes a brief presentation to the group on their collage. At the conclusion of the presentations, the group is asked to reflect on how the activity (a) helped them to know this student better and (b) helped them to know themselves as teachers better.

6. Participants are then instructed to place the poster prominently on display in their classrooms without any word of explanation to the class and make silent, regular reference to it throughout the rest of the school year.

Teachers who have not participated in the Unmasking Success activity may ask whether, with a class of twenty-five students, it is realistic to expect a teacher to spend so much time understanding just one student. We would respond that teacher self-knowledge and craft improvement, more often than not, comes through focusing on the work of one student and is generally applicable to larger groups of students. Langer and

Colton (2005) confirm this observation in an article on the collaborative analysis of student work:

> Collaborative inquiry is most instructive when teachers narrow their study to the complexities and uncertainties of one student's learning. . . . Because the focus students [more often than not] represent a cluster of students who exhibit similar learning challenges, teachers can use what they learn from studying one student with the larger group. (p. 23)

The knowledge is meaningful and relevant because it is specific, transferable, and can be generalized.

MAPPING OUR PROFESSIONAL SELVES

Segmentation is a powerful tool that is used in many industries and businesses as a means to support critical thinking and analysis about complex and often seemingly contradictory issues. It is, however, not often used in education but has great potential for assisting us as we come to know more about our profession and our professional selves.

In essence, segmentation is a tool for analysis. Two critical dimensions of an issue are plotted on vertical and horizontal axes (see Figure 3.1). Thus the graphic organizer creates four distinct quadrants. For example, we could choose to explore two relatively straightforward attributes of teacher instructional behavior: *organization* and *efficacy*. We might put teacher *organization* on the vertical axis as a continuum from highly organized to highly disorganized. In the same way, we might put teacher *efficacy* on the horizontal axis. The segmentation might look something like Figure 3.1.

The next step in segmentation is to write descriptors in the four quadrants. For example, in Figure 3.1 we asked ourselves what might be some of the characteristics of a teacher with a high degree of organization and planning but a low degree of efficacy. We thought of two general categories: the first category is the enthusiastic beginner (the teacher fresh from teacher training college) who has enormous enthusiasm and passion but not a great deal of self-confidence. The second category might be the highly experienced, but disillusioned, "pro" who may be suffering from teacher burnout (the teacher who still plans meticulously, perhaps out of habit or a sense of duty, but is

Figure 3.1 Segmentation Template

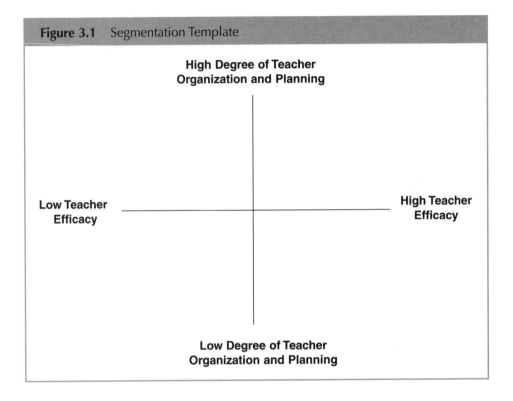

pessimistic about whether the instruction will have any real impact or influence upon students).

Possible dimensions for such segmentation could include attributes such as *teacher optimism* and *expectations* or *teacher emotional self-regulation* and *student trust*. The dimensions can be any two interrelated characteristics of teaching and learning. During the summers, Bill teaches a course at the Principals' Training Center (PTC) for aspiring administrators in which he uses segmentation to explore the relationships in school leadership between task and relationship orientation, vision and practical implementation skills, and ethical behavior and courage.

We have included our model of the organization and efficacy segmentation with some descriptors inserted into each of the quadrants (see Figure 3.2).

The value of the segmentation exercise is enhanced by selecting attributes of teaching and learning that are personally relevant and meaningful. You would then write the quadrant descriptors out of personal experience. The next step is to plot in the four quadrants where you presently are and where you would like to be. The final step is to analyze what needs to happen to make the journey between "where I am" and "where I would like to be." The process makes us reflect on our classroom experiences and strongly encourages professional introspection.

Figure 3.2 Segmentation: Organization Versus Efficacy

High Degree of Teacher Organization and Planning

- Teacher's careful planning may be sabotaged by low self-confidence and low expectations of students.
- Teacher may be burned out, pessimistic, and cynical.
- Teacher may send mixed messages; students are confused.
- Teacher may be an enthusiastic beginner.
- Although teacher may have very carefully thought through lesson plans, lack of self-confidence may create classroom-management issues that prevent the plan from being implemented.
- Teacher may attempt to substitute autocratic rule in the classroom in place of developing constructive learning relationships.

- Teacher develops clear learning objectives and strategies designed to achieve them.
- Teacher's verbal and nonverbal communication is congruent and provides students with a single message.
- Teacher is optimistic and has high expectations of students and self.
- Teacher models responsible and responsive follow-through and expects the same from students.
- Teacher is resilient and seeks multiple ways to ensure student success.
- Teacher is open to new ideas.
- Teacher seeks feedback from students on instruction.

Low Teacher Efficacy

- This may be the 'burned out' teacher who has become apathetic.
- Stress may create a sense of "learned helplessness."
- Teacher often acts as though "one size fits all" and is quick to dismiss exceptional students as incorrigible.
- Instruction is workbook or textbook driven.
- Teacher does not like change or innovation.
- Teacher finds feedback threatening and is reluctant to seek it.
- This teacher lacks resilience and is quick to give up on students and self.

- Classroom is characterized by a high degree of spontaneity, but assessment of student learning is random and haphazard.
- Teacher easily drifts off topic.
- Lessons may have considerable entertainment value, but probably do not have clearly defined or assessable learning objectives.
- This may be a popular, charismatic teacher with a broad repertoire of high-interest stories.
- This teacher may not budget time wisely, may get bogged down and fail to finish the syllabus.
- Teacher may embrace too much innovation (flavor-of-the-month syndrome) without the perseverance or organization to develop necessary skills.

High Teacher Efficacy

Low Degree of Teacher Organization and Planning

SOLICITING FEEDBACK FROM OUR STUDENTS

If professional self-knowledge is critical to building constructive learning relationships in the classroom, it becomes self-evident that teachers must seek information on how they are being perceived by their students.

It continues to surprise us how many highly experienced teachers are reluctant to ask students for such feedback. For some, the resistance may be predicated on the assumptions that it is often the teachers' responsibility to make unpopular decisions, to correct inappropriate behavior, to set limits, and to insist upon high standards and that these aspects of their classroom work will produce some predictable, negative student responses. Sometimes this may be true. However, our experience suggests that the vast majority of students are fair-minded and often share remarkably valuable observations and insights. Most students, even primary school–aged children, are able to separate who the teacher is from the various roles the teacher may occupy in the classroom.

When we conduct teacher-training workshops, we ask for participant feedback at the close of each day. The feedback can be either oral or written. If we are conducting it orally, we will often use a "plusses and wishes" format. Plusses (aspects of the training that have worked well for the participants) are scribed onto a flipchart. Then the wishes (what the participants would like to see changed for the following day) are scribed onto the flipchart. The flipchart containing the plusses and wishes is posted in the training room for the remainder of the workshop or course so that we can make easy reference to it.

If the feedback is written, we will often limit it to two or three specific questions. For example, "What major learnings did I take away from today's session?" "How was the pacing of today's workshop?" or "What advice would I like to give to the trainers?" (Another way of framing the last question is to provide "stop-start-continue" sentence stem completions: "The trainers should stop . . ." "The trainers should start . . ." "The trainers should continue . . .")

Ochan and her teaching partner, Alex Smith, often framed an "exit card" question for their Grade 8 humanities students around an innovation that they were experimenting with in the classroom. A couple of years ago, Ochan and Alex introduced "warm-ups" at the start of each lesson. The warm-ups were short, highly interactive, and engaging activities that were connected to the central theme or objective of the specific lesson. Ochan and Alex had a hunch that these warm-ups would help the students focus their attention and concentration faster than if they simply went directly into the content of the lesson. After several weeks of using daily warm-ups, they sought written feedback from the students. Their hunch was borne out in spades. The students overwhelmingly reported that they appreciated the interactive introduction to the lessons and their exit cards included numerous comments such as "the warm-ups really help me to wake up my brain."

We like to use the "making thinking visual" strategy for exit cards in which the participants or students complete two sentence stems: "I used to think . . ." and "Now, I think . . ."

Feedback on Feedback

In either an adult workshop or a classroom situation it is very useful to give feedback on feedback. This is when the teacher takes a few minutes to summarize to the class the feedback that was received from the students. This accomplishes three important functions. First, it lets the students know that their comments are being taken seriously by the teacher. It is empowering and so encourages students to be thoughtful when they write future observations and comments. Second, it models for the students that their teacher is a lifelong learner who is seeking to improve. Third, it builds trust between the teacher and the students.

CASE STUDY

Directions: Please read the case study below and address the discussion questions that follow.

"Moths and Monkeys, Cabbages and Kings"

"I think it's important for teachers to select topics to teach that they are enthusiastic about." Grace spoke for the first time during the meeting of second-grade teachers. Grace was assigned to Grade 2 as the learning specialist for students with special needs.

"But we can't seem to agree on what topics we are going to cover in science," Adam repeated unnecessarily. Adam was the frustrated peacemaker. "I still think that there is room for compromise. I can think of some great activities dealing with moths . . ."

"We have always done green plants early in the second term," Melody Sykes argued. She had been at the school for 15 years. "The children look forward to it. Anyway, I've already purchased the seeds and the paper cups. Why change just for the sake of change?"

"I don't think moths or green plants are the issue at all," Marvel Brumby murmured. She had spoken louder earlier in the meeting but had been interrupted by Melody. "I don't care if we teach cabbages or kings."

"I don't think that's a very positive attitude," Melody grumbled. "Why are you always so negative?"

"I'm not negative," Marvel protested. "But topics don't matter. What matters are the reasons behind our selection."

"You may not think you're negative," Melody announced. "But just look at the effect on the rest of us. Every time we sit down to collaborate together, you come up with some obstacle to our work together."

"Do we all have to teach the same topics?" Adam asked. Anything to stop the bickering, anything to avoid conflict.

"The children like green plants," Melody repeated herself. "They get really excited about watching the seeds sprout. We even have growing races between the beans. I award a blue ribbon to the fastest growing bean."

"I think it's only fair that I'm given equal time for moths," Ryan Crumble announced. "Frankly, I don't think there is any comparison in terms of student interest. Think of the dynamic life cycle of a moth."

"Grace could design some beautiful bulletin boards about moths," Mildred Bucklesford added.

"We'd be playing to our strengths as a team," Adam contributed. "Grace does brilliant bulletin boards."

"I vote for monkeys," Marvel Brumby announced fiercely.

"Why monkeys? We haven't been talking about monkeys. Why would anyone want to study monkeys?" Melody retorted.

"Exactly!" Marvel announced and grinned at the puzzled faces that surrounded her. "Why would anyone want to study monkeys or moths or green plants?"

"Why won't you join the team, Marvel? Why are you always so contrary?" Melody asked rhetorically.

"If we shortened the units a little, we could do both green plants and moths," Adam suggested. "There's nothing to stop us from compromising. Grace could do alternate bulletin boards. It could be a win-win situation. Everyone wins . . ."

"Except the kids," Marvel said under her breath.

Discussion Questions

1. What are some of the assumptions in the case study?

2. What negative presuppositions exist in this case study? How might they be linked to perceptions, expectations, and attributions?

3. At what point does the conflict become personalized?

4. If you were the chair at the next meeting, how might you proceed?

4 Taming the Beast

Teacher Self-Management

The teaching profession expects and demands that teachers be emotionally self-regulating—at least as far as the more extreme manifestations of emotions are concerned. But it is often subtle failures of emotional self-regulation that are the most destructive. A teacher who employs belittling sarcasm in the classroom can be much more harmful than one who occasionally displays a loss of temper. In some cases, teachers may not even be aware of the failure of self-regulation.

MICHAEL'S ASPIRATION

Take, for example, the case of Michael in his first month in the ninth grade. During an English class discussion on educational goals, Michael volunteered that one of his aspirations was to undertake the International Baccalaureate Diploma Program. His teacher turned to him with a quizzical look and said "You?" Michael was devastated. For days that grew into weeks he was depressed and listless. He lost interest in academic work, especially in English. He stopped attending extracurricular activities and seemed indifferent to his friendship circle. Fortunately, his mother and his previous year's teacher saw the change in Michael and intervened to bolster his seriously injured self-confidence.

Michael's English teacher was not a vicious or mean-spirited woman. She has children of her own, and we suspect she had no intention of wounding her student. However, her inability to control her impulsiveness and empathize with Michael created a serious crisis for one young man.

Impulse control is a critical dimension of self-management. It allows us to delay gratification and anticipate consequences. These are the bedrock of long-term planning and achievement motivation. We can project our possible behaviors into the future and anticipate outcomes. Experimental research (Goleman, 1995) has shown that students who master a degree of impulse control are more academically and socially competent than those who act on whim. A marvelously simple experiment illustrates the remarkable predictive power of delayed gratification.

THE MARSHMALLOW CHALLENGE

Self-imposed delay of gratification is the essence of emotional self-regulation and self-control and is a direct determinant of how well or how poorly people are able to use their other intellectual talents. In the 1960s, Stanford University psychologist Walter Mischel conducted a now-famous research experiment at a nearby preschool (Shoda, Mischel, & Peake, 1990). The study then tracked the four-year-olds over the next fourteen years until they graduated from high school.

The research design was simple: The four-year-olds were given a proposal. They could have one marshmallow immediately. It was placed on the table before them. But if they were able to wait until the researcher had run a short errand, they could have two marshmallows. In other words, those four-year-olds who were unable to delay gratification could have a single marshmallow immediately, but those preschoolers who were able to wait for a few minutes could have two marshmallows. Goleman (1995) writes that it was a "challenge sure to try the soul of any four-year-old, a microcosm of the eternal battle between impulse and restraint, id and ego, desire and self-control, gratification and delay. Which of these choices a child makes is a telling test; it offers a quick reading not just of character, but of the trajectory that the child will probably make through life" (p. 81).

Predictably, some of the four-year-olds who underwent the marshmallow challenge were unable to resist temptation. More impulsive, they grabbed the single marshmallow and scoffed it down almost within seconds of when the researcher left the room. But others were able to delay gratification.

The predictive and diagnostic power of the marshmallow challenge only became evident some twelve to fourteen years later when these same children were tracked as adolescents. The difference between the two groups in terms of social and emotional development was dramatic. Those who had been able to delay gratification at the age of four were "more socially competent; personally effective, self-assertive and better able to cope with the frustrations of life. They were less likely to go to pieces, freeze or regress under stress, or become rattled and disorganized when pressured; they embraced challenges and pursued them instead of giving up in the face of difficulties" (p. 81).

Phil Peake (as cited in Goleman, 1995), a research psychologist at Smith College, carried the analysis of the marshmallow data into an academic context and arrived at some startling conclusions. Peake evaluated these young people as they finished secondary school. Those who had been able to resist the marshmallow temptation at the age of four were "far superior as students to those who had acted upon whim. . . . They were more academically competent: better able to put ideas into words, to use and respond to reason, to concentrate . . . more eager to learn" (p. 82). Peake found a dramatic correlation between preschool impulse control and high school SAT scores. The group who had resisted temptation at the age of four scored significantly higher, over one hundred points on both the Verbal and Quantitative sections respectively, and over two hundred points higher on the total SAT score.

The research results suggest a strong correlation between impulse control and perseverance: the capacity to put aside immediate frustrations for the prospect of a larger and longer-term goal (Powell, 1998).

The benefits of self-awareness and self-regulation are not limited to students in school but also play a critical role in professional collaboration between teachers.

MARGARET: THE LOOSE CANNON

A decade or so ago a prominent international school in Asia implemented the concept of *learning communities* in its middle school. The core academic teachers were clustered into teams that met regularly to develop common unit plans, exchange ideas on effective instructional strategies, and collaborate in common assessments of student work. After only a few weeks of the new structure, the middle school principal was profoundly worried about the sixth-grade team. "It wasn't really a team at all. It was a group of individuals that met weekly to engage in verbal combat. Not only was student learning not being addressed, but teacher relationships were deteriorating—big time!"

The principal had a private meeting with the sixth-grade team leader, and together they traced the root of the team's dysfunction to the participation of a single member: Margaret.

Margaret was an effective classroom teacher who seemed much more comfortable and self-confident in the company of children than adults. She was generally liked and respected by her students, and their parents had no complaints about the instruction their children were receiving. However, when it came to the weekly team meetings, Margaret was perceived by her colleagues as defensive, stubborn, inflexible, disruptive, and volatile. On several occasions, she had taken an innocuous comment personally and had "lost it" with fellow team members. One other member of the team had stopped participating in meetings because of the potential for conflict.

The sixth-grade team leader was particularly distraught about Margaret's behavior at these meetings because she counted Margaret as a personal friend. The team leader agreed that she would meet with Margaret and develop a plan for improving the interaction at team meetings. The first step was getting Margaret to understand how she might be contributing to the team's difficulties. The team leader anticipated that this would be the most difficult part of their conversation. She predicted that Margaret would either deny that anything was wrong ("There's nothing wrong with a little professional disagreement") or blame the others for the destructive interaction.

She was wrong. As soon as the topic of the team meetings was broached, Margaret burst into tears! "I know I'm part of the problem," she admitted. "It's just really hard not to take some of the things that are said personally." Margaret had managed to develop some accurate *declarative knowledge* of the difficult situation, but did not as yet possess the *procedural knowledge* necessary to do anything about it. She had a degree of self-awareness, but not yet the self-regulation that would allow her to manage relationships constructively.

Over the weeks to come, Margaret and her team leader developed a four-point plan to improve Margaret's participation in team meetings:

1. *Anticipate "hot button" responses.* Margaret was encouraged to identify, in advance, situations, comments, and the nonverbal behavior of her colleagues that was likely to trigger a volatile response within her. She was reminded not to fall into the "default" position of assuming that criticism was the same as an attack. She was encouraged to monitor closely her physiological reactions in team meetings and attempt to disengage herself emotionally from the content of the conversations.

2. *Practice and rehearse.* The team leader spent a few minutes each week going over with Margaret in advance the agenda of their team meetings. She provided Margaret with an opportunity to practice constructive reactions to potentially volatile situations and rehearse those responses.

3. *Role-play.* When difficult topics or conversations were on the horizon, Margaret and her team leader would actually take a few minutes ahead of the meeting to engage in structured role-play.

4. *Use external clueing.* Margaret and her team leader developed a secret visual code through which the team leader could signal her when she perceived Margaret's behavior becoming inflexible or overly reactive.

In this way, over time, Margaret was able to translate the declarative knowledge of self-awareness into the procedural knowledge of self-regulation that actually made a difference in team meetings. Her colleagues were quick to notice the effort that Margaret was making, and they went out of their way to support her.

Obviously, it was not always smooth sailing; however, two years later when the sixth-grade team leader was retiring from the school, she recommended to the principal that Margaret be appointed as her replacement as team leader. The principal did so with the full support of the other team members. Margaret's continued self-regulation had made her as effective in team meetings as she was in the classroom.

There can be little doubt that self-regulation is influenced by culture. Some cultures reward extroverted self-expression of emotions, while others seem to value a more reserved stoicism. However the manifestation, all cultures expect some degree of self-regulation. Without it, we could not develop community.

Self-aware and self-regulating individuals tend to have an internal locus of responsibility and are intrinsically motivated by deeply held values. They are subject to impulsive feelings and distressing emotions but are able to manage them well. They stay composed and unflappable even in highly stressful moments. They do not yield to the temptation of negativity, and they think clearly and stay focused under pressure. They are autonomous individuals and yet work well in teams. They have a profound sense of optimism and hope.

Teachers who have emotional self-control are more able to stay focused on issues that are truly important. This makes them more likely to be conscientious, to meet commitments and keep promises. Teachers who self-regulate are more likely to hold themselves accountable for realizing personal and school goals. Self-regulating teachers are more organized, methodical, and meticulous in their work.

Teachers who have self-control are aware of the past, present, and future without being a prisoner to any of them. For this reason they tend to be more adaptable, able to handle multiple demands and changing priorities. They are tolerant of ambiguity and adapt their response behaviors to match specific circumstances. They are flexible in their thinking and able to generate fresh perspectives. They are also innovative, seeking out new ideas and original approaches to knotty problems.

THE PLEASURE PRINCIPLE

Sigmund Freud (1930/1989) suggested that our primal motivation is to seek pleasure and avoid pain. While subsequent research in psychology and neuroscience suggests that human motivation may be more complex than just this, the quest for pleasure and the avoidance of pain certainly play central roles in our classrooms.

Teachers who have self-awareness and self-management are more able to make learning pleasurable for their students, and pleasure is essential to meaningful learning. When a child returns home from school in the afternoon and announces that "I didn't learn anything" during the school day and that the class is "boring," it may be just a knee-jerk response to the mother's habitual question: "What did you learn in school today?" However, it may also be that the child is genuinely bored by repetitive drills, fragmented memorization, and learning that seems irrelevant and meaningless. The imposition of such so-called learning is not only not pleasurable, but it is tedious mental torture that in all honesty can be likened to intellectual child abuse. Teachers with intellectual and emotional empathy for their students avoid such practices.

The pleasure principle is controlled by the neurotransmitter dopamine. When we experience the intellectual joy of making a new and surprising connection between ideas, a small surge of dopamine is released in the brain. This creates the pleasurable sensation that we associate with "hot cognition"—the excitement of discovery. The release of dopamine creates a somatovisceral reaction, a cognitive thrill that resonates throughout our bodies. Such release of dopamine is addictive and is the foundation of lifelong learning.

Student pleasure in the classroom can be greatly influence by teacher behavior. Teachers can plan intellectual challenges that will actively engage students. They can mediate relevance. They can answer explicitly the question: Why is this important for students to know or do?

Perhaps the highest form of self-management is when we think of it not simply as a restraining force on volatile or destructive emotions but also as the genesis of positive learning-enhancing behavior on the part of the teacher, for example, when teachers take an intellectual risk and model the excitement and thrill of learning in front of their students. This implies that the teacher arrives in the classroom "unprepared"—without all the right answers—and engages with the students in genuine intellectual exploration. When teachers engage in their own learning in front of their students, a powerful authenticity is created. Enthusiasm and excitement are created. Dopamine is released, and learning becomes meaningful and pleasurable.

SELF-REGULATION AND TRUST

Teacher self-management lends itself to trustworthiness. When teachers stay composed and unflappable, thinking clearly while under pressure, they generate a classroom climate of trustworthiness. Students perceive them to be reliable and predictable. They are not caught up in the powerful winds of volatile emotions. The leader of the classroom has a steady hand on the tiller.

By controlling impulsivity, teachers are able to avoid the temptation of acting upon destructive emotions. We are able to connect with our deeply held values and so act with sensitivity, honesty, and integrity. Self-regulation also allows us to admit our own mistakes and shortcomings and appropriately confront unethical behavior in others.

WHEN DOES SELF-CONTROL BECOME SELF-DEFEATING?

Those of us who work in service occupations (such as teaching, social work, and nursing) perform physical, intellectual, and emotional labor. Emotional labor is when we deliberately control our emotions and their expression in our behavior to conform to the external expectations of the workplace. We see emotional labor when the server at McDonald's gives us a broad smile and says "Have a nice day." We see emotional labor when the hospital nurse hides his frustration with a difficult patient and remains outwardly caring and compassionate. We see emotional labor when the police officer remains calm and professional in the face of an irate driver who is receiving a speeding ticket.

Emotional labor involves self-control and self-regulation. We are called upon to "act" in a way that may be contrary to how we are actually feeling at the time. Psychologists have identified two types of emotional labor: *surface acting* and *deep acting*.

Let's examine how these two types of emotional labor may play out in two classic films:

1. In 1976, Francois Truffaut released a wonderful film titled *Small Change*. It is a delightful study of resilient children in a French village. Toward the end of the film, a veteran teacher of a small provincial school is interviewed about her life's work. The interviewer recognizes her many, many years of devoted service to children in the classroom and comments that she must like children very much. "To the contrary," she replies. She doesn't like children at all. She shrugs in a very French, noncommittal manner and dismisses her long service to *les enfants* as an unpleasant but necessary duty.

2. Contrast her reaction to the response of the young substitute teacher in Zhang Yimou's 2000 film *Not One Less*. In the crushing poverty of rural China, thirteen-year-old Wei is ordered to a remote village to be a substitute teacher in a one-room schoolhouse. Barely older than her students, the shy girl is charged with keeping the class intact for one month or she won't be paid. At first Wei is bitter and takes very little interest in her charges. She simply writes the lessons on the blackboard and spends the rest of the time moping outside. However, in time we see Wei emerge as a self-confident and committed teacher who genuinely cares about her students. The turning point of the film comes when the number one troublemaker in the class runs away to the city to find work. The teacher, however, is determined to follow the boy and bring him back to school. Once in the city, her simple peasant pleas fall on deaf ears, and only when the local television station sympathizes does her search bear fruit.

From the comments of the veteran school teacher in Truffaut's (1976) *Small Change,* we might suspect that for at least some of her long career she was engaged in surface acting, in which there was a lack of alignment not only between her felt emotions and her behavior but also between her behavior and her deeply held beliefs. Having said that, the French veteran's comment about a "sense of duty" does suggest some deep acting in the sense that she may have been acting in accordance with her social values.

In Zhang Yimou's (2000) film, young Wei is able to overcome her bitterness and depression and she emerges as a teacher capable of deep acting. Although her felt emotions and her behavior may not be aligned (she may be very angry but does not show it), her behavior is congruent with her values of compassion and caring.

In short, emotional labor is when employees regulate their public displays of emotion to comply with certain external expectations (Barsade & Gibson, 2007). An employee's felt emotions can differ quite dramatically from displayed emotions. Different workplaces have different "display rules" for employee demonstrations of emotion. Part of our daily professional performance is almost certainly surface acting. This is when the tired and stressed-out principal forces a smile and acts with friendliness toward an angry and unreasonable parent. Surface acting is in contrast to deep acting in which the principal is able to depersonalize the situation, cultivate the detachment necessary to see that the parent is attempting to advocate (albeit inappropriately) for the child, and express empathy. In deep acting, the principal's behaviors and values align, though behaviors and emotions may not.

The difference between surface acting and deep acting may be a contributing factor to teacher stress and ultimate burn out. Surface acting may result in "emotional dissonance" and contribute to work strain, anxiety, and depression. Barsade and Gibson (2007) suggest that deep acting may be healthier because it causes less stress and burnout, particularly the emotional exhaustion caused from having to control one's emotions and play a role.

Bob Ames (as cited in Nieto, 2005) writes about how surface acting and deep acting can affect both student and teacher behaviors:

> Teaching is an interactive, interpersonal experience that requires personality and communication. Initially, I tried to emulate the methods of my colleagues and I failed miserably. . . . Teaching is based on trust, and when students see me as a real person who genuinely wants them to succeed, strong bonds are formed. On the other hand, if I'm "acting" as the teacher, the kids "act" as students and a host of stereotypical behaviors present themselves. (p. 37)

IF TEACHING INVOLVES ACTING, WHAT DOES THE AUDIENCE THINK?

What do students thinks about teacher emotional intelligence? What are the teacher self-management qualities that promote student learning?

In 1997, Jean Rudduck, Julia Day, and Gwen Wallace in the United Kingdom examined student views of schooling and school improvement initiatives. They interviewed more than eight hundred secondary school students and looked for common responses to the question: "What are the characteristics of teachers who are most likely to increase student commitment to learning?" They identified ten features of teacher behaviors and attitudes that students frequently associated with increased learning. Interestingly enough, it would appear that what the students knew intuitively about the effective classroom has been to a large extent borne out in recent research: The emotional regulation of the teacher is critical to creating a classroom climate conducive to learning.

What follows below are the attributes identified by the students of teachers most likely to increase student commitment to learning. Notice how many are connected to emotional intelligence and specifically to teacher emotional self-regulation (Rudduck et al., 1997):

> Teachers most likely to increase student commitment to learning are those who
>
> - Enjoy teaching the subject
> - Enjoy teaching students
> - Make lessons interesting and link them to life outside school
> - Will have a laugh but know how to keep order
> - Are fair
> - Are easy for students to talk to
> - Don't shout
> - Don't go on about things (e.g., how much better the other classes are, how much better an older brother or sister was)
> - Explain things and go through things students don't understand without making them feel small
> - Don't give up on students (p. 86)

Lisa Delpit (Cushman, 2003) had eighth- and ninth-grade students write a teacher job description. Interestingly, the students focused almost exclusively on aspects of teacher emotional intelligence, particularly on areas of self-management: "Must have a sense of humor; must not make students feel bad about themselves; must be fair . . . must not jump to conclusions; must let students know them; must get to know students; must not scream; must be patient . . . must be able to listen, even when mad" (p. xv).

When we think about it, there are few job descriptions that are as emotionally complex and demanding as that of a teacher.

THE SPARK BEFORE THE FLAME: EMOTIONAL AWARENESS AND MANAGEMENT

Self-regulation allows us to be social, which is arguably the most distinguishing feature of our human species. Socializing is not a mere pleasant pastime. It is an evolutionary and psychological necessity. Social isolation can be debilitating both psychologically and physiologically. House,

Landis, and Umberson (1988) suggest that social isolation is as physiologically harmful as smoking or high blood pressure. Fear of rejection is one of the most profound and widespread anxieties experienced across all cultures. Eisenberger and Lieberman (2004) suggest that this fear is primordial in that in human prehistory membership in a band was necessary for survival and rejection was tantamount to a death sentence. Think of our prison system. Short of capital punishment, the most severe consequence for misbehavior is solitary confinement. Our profound need to be social makes it imperative that our emotions do not run amok.

To exert control over an emotion, we must first be aware of it. Ekman (Dalai Lama & Ekman, 2008) suggests that many emotions come upon us unawares. In other words, we actually come under the influence of the emotion without being consciously aware of feeling it. Think of the times that we have witnessed another person grow irritated. At a certain point in the conversation, we paraphrase the person's emotion to them: "You're feeling very frustrated about . . ." Often the response is a pause, a glimmer of recognition, perhaps even surprise, and then confirmation: "Yes, I am feeling *very frustrated* . . ." On other occasions, the response may be an even more irritable denial: "I'm not angry. What makes you think I'm angry?" In both cases, there is the suggestion that the individuals are at least initially unaware of the emotions that are influencing them.

Paraphrasing of emotion, as described in the previous paragraph, can literally forge a communication pathway between the limbic system and the neocortex.

So the first step in emotional self-regulation is to become aware of the emotion we are feeling before giving way to the impulse to act upon it. This is what Ekman (Dalai Lama & Ekman, 2008) refers to as apprehending the "spark before the flame" (p. 42). In Eastern Buddhism the process is called "mindfulness" or "meta-attention" (p. 23), and there is research to support the notion that practice in meditation can actually increase our awareness of our emotions. "Most people, unless they engage in a lot of meditative practice, . . . have no conscious recognition that an impulse or spark has arisen before they engage in emotional behavior, the flame" (p. 44).

EMOTIONAL MANAGEMENT

Plutchik (1994) has identified four basic emotional dichotomies: anger and fear, joy and sadness, acceptance and disgust, and surprise and anticipation. In each coupling, one emotion is the opposite of the other. He has taken an evolutionary approach and perceives that within each dichotomy there are aspects of the emotional range that lend themselves to our survival as a species. However, the fight-or-flight response of our cave-dwelling ancestor may be entirely inappropriate to our work in classrooms. It is useful to look at some specific emotions and how their self-regulation plays out in teaching.

Probably the emotion that comes to mind first when we think about self-control is anger. Anger is one of the most challenging emotions that teachers are called upon to manage. It is challenging because it releases chemicals that both attract and repel us. Anger can be seductive, luring us into impulsive and irrational behavior that we later come to regret. Anger can also cause us to feel nauseated. Depending upon how anger is managed, it can be either useful and productive in the classroom or highly destructive. The difference may have to do with the teacher's ability to engage in deep acting.

When negative, disruptive emotions intrude into the classroom, learning suffers. More often than not, outbursts of frustration and anger on the part of the teacher are perceived as highly threatening to the child and result in what Paul MacLean (1990) refers to as *downshifting* in which our basic fight, flight, or freeze instincts are evoked. In such a state, risk taking and creativity are greatly inhibited and higher-level thinking is virtually impossible.

We would argue that there is a place for carefully managed anger in the classroom, but we would counsel that it is only constructive under some very specific conditions. First, it is rarely advisable to express anger when we are actually in the grip of it. And second, the anger needs to focus on the objectionable action, not the actor.

In his *Nichomachean Ethics*, Aristotle (trans. 2006) writes: "Anyone can become angry—that is easy. But to be angry with the right person, to the right degree, at the right time, for the right purpose and in the right way—that is not easy."

ANGER AND EMPATHY: A BRIDGE JUMPER GETS A PUSH

Anger can distort our perceptions and make empathy impossible as illustrated in the following story (BBC World Service News, 2009):

On May 23, 2009, Chen Fuchao climbed to the top of the Haizhu Bridge in Guangzhou, China, and threatened to commit suicide by jumping. He announced that he was desperate after a failed construction project had left him deeply in debt.

Traffic on the bridge was stopped for five hours while the police attempted to coax Mr. Chen to safety. Finally, Lai Jiansheng, a stranded motorist on the bridge, broke through the police cordon, climbed to where Mr. Chen sat, pretended to shake hands with him, and then pushed him off the edge.

Mr. Lai said he was very angry with the "selfish activity" of the would-be jumper. "I pushed him off because jumpers like Chen are very selfish. . . . Their action violates a lot of public interest. They do not dare to kill themselves. Instead they just want to raise the relevant government authorities to their appeals" (BBC World Service News, para. 11–12).

Mr. Lai's anger had blinded him to empathy and caused him to concoct a very shallow interpretation of Mr. Chen's motives.

Note: Fortunately, Mr. Chen landed on a partially filled air mattress and was taken to a local hospital with only minor injuries (BBC World Service News).

TEACHER ANGER IN THE CLASSROOM

For teachers, it is rarely a good idea to demonstrate anger in the classroom when we are still in the grip of feeling it. This is where deep acting comes into play. In deep acting, our behavior may not reflect our felt emotions but is congruent with our values. If a child has misbehaved, it may be appropriate for the teacher to express disappointment. There may be some anger in his tone of voice (although he may actually feel little at the time of the interchange). The critical issue is that the anger is present for the benefit of correcting the child's behavior—not simply as a means of giving vent to our personal frustration.

A number of years ago, we worked with a colleague who was chronically unable to control his temper. There were frequent outbursts of frustration and anger in his classroom, and the students came to expect this behavior from him. At first, the lack of emotional self-regulation intimidated and frightened the students. But as time went by, this teacher became the object of his students' secret ridicule and they sought deliberately to provoke such outbursts. On one notable occasion, a group of students actually visited his home and stole his underwear from the washing line in order to orchestrate yet another outburst. Ironically, the locus of the teacher's emotional control had shifted from himself to his students.

On the other hand, we once worked with a masterful middle school principal who opened a brand new computer writing lab only to discover that some of the students had stolen all the marbles out of the computer mice. He summoned the middle school students into an assembly and deliberately and firmly let the students perceive his anger and disappointment. He announced that the computer lab would remain closed until all the marbles were returned. The marbles reappeared within forty-eight hours.

THE MOST DESTRUCTIVE EMOTION: CONTEMPT

In *Thus Spake Zarathustra,* Friedrich Nietzsche (1916) advanced his belief that one does not hate what one can despise. Far more problematic than teacher anger in the classroom is any display of contempt. The psychologist John Gottman (as cited in Gladwell, 2005) has worked for many years to map the verbal and nonverbal behavior of married couples in conflict situations. He invites couples to his so-called love lab, puts them into a conflict situation, and videotapes the interaction. His research assistants then "map" the exchange. Gottman and his team have identified more than forty different behavioral manifestations of emotional states, and from a less-than-fifteen-minute video, Gottman can predict with over 90 percent accuracy whether the marriage will survive. One of the most powerful indicators of a soon-to-fail marriage, according to Gottman, is the presence of behavior that suggests contempt. Contempt does not need to be expressed verbally. It can be is a dismissive look, scornfully-raised eyebrows, the rolling of the eyes, or a sarcastic tone of voice.

Unlike anger, contempt indicates that the victim has little or no value in our eyes and is unworthy of our serious attention. Contempt does not attempt to change behavior or promote student learning. On the contrary, it savagely attacks the victim's sense of self-worth. It is often a prelude to social exclusion and can be extremely contagious. It is not hard to recall times in which the teacher's scorn of a particular student was continued by classmates during recess or after school. Contempt heralds a complete absence of respect and caring. It is immensely destructive to the fragile relationship between student and teacher.

The facial expressions that we associate with contempt are often similar to those we employ when feeling disgust.

PRIDE GOETH BEFORE THE FALL

On the other hand, the Dalai Lama (Dalai Lama & Ekman, 2008) questions whether contempt is not distorted pride.

Pride is a curious emotion and the feelings we have about it are connected to the language we use to describe it. In the West we have a love-hate relationship with pride. We recognize pride as one of the seven deadly sins. We recall that Satan was expelled from heaven for the sin of pride, and we talk about "pride going before the fall." We see this negative perception of pride in expressions of arrogance, contempt, and condescension. In its negative manifestation, teacher pride may be associated with self-aggrandizing, ego-enhancing displays of power and erudition.

However, pride can also be a powerful energy source and motivator. How many times have we exhorted our students to take pride in their work? We certainly want them to value a sense of achievement. As teachers, we also take professional pride in our craftsmanship. It is our ongoing determination to improve our craft as educators that keeps professional development on the front burners of most schools.

We also take pride in the accomplishments of our students. Unfortunately, there is no word in English for this kind of pride. In Yiddish it is called *naches*—the specific, selfless pleasure that a teacher (or parent) takes in the success of students. In our experience, this is the greatest source of teacher satisfaction and the greatest motivator in an underpaid and underappreciated profession.

JOY AND SORROW

On either side of the majestic entrance to the Kraton, the Sultan's palace in Yogjakarta, Indonesia, there are two fifteen-feet-high stone statues of warriors brandishing swords. One is said to represent the forces of good and the other the forces of evil. But the guide isn't sure which is which because the statues are identical. The message is presumably that distinguishing between good and evil can be a tricky business. The same, we believe, can be said for joy and sorrow.

Joy and sorrow need and rely upon each other. We come to know one through our knowledge of the other. We also often experience them simultaneously. When we come to the end of a school year with a class that we have greatly enjoyed teaching, we experience not only the joy of a year's professional and personal fulfillment but also the grief and sorrow that the class will soon move on to a different teacher.

Our experiences of joy are often spontaneous and short lived. They provide us with powerful emotional memories and the desire to recapture that intense pleasure in the future. One particular type of joy is the stimulating pleasure we experience when we make new intellectual connections, when we solve complex problems, or when we make new discoveries. These joyous cognitive moments are ephemeral, but they provide for the motivation for future learning.

However, if you ask people to identify the greatest learning experiences of their lives, the chances are good that they will *not* select an experience of joy or intense pleasure. More often than not, they will select an event or situation that was traumatic, challenging, involved prolonged hardship, or produced feelings of failure, guilt, or regret. You may hear about the serious illness or death of a loved one, a painful divorce, a teenager alienated from parents, a failure in business or school, or perhaps a ruptured friendship. Each of these difficult situations can produce powerful emotions and the possibility of deep and insightful learning.

Ask teachers which class has represented for them the greatest personal learning experience, and the chances are good they will recall a challenging, difficult class that may have caused them considerable anxiety and anguish.

Sorrow and sadness have a longer lasting effect upon us than joy, and perhaps, ironically, there is much greater potential for learning that can emanate from a sad situation than from a joyous one. However, we can only learn from sorrow if we appropriately attribute our sense of regret.

RICHARD'S NEED FOR A SANDWICH

Early in his teaching career Bill taught at a school for young adults who were emotionally disturbed and learning disabled in the suburbs of New York City. Richard, a fifteen-year-old muscle builder, joined Bill's class in November. He had been expelled from public schools for his uncontrolled temper that had led to violence against teachers and other students. Richard was on probation from the juvenile courts.

Richard also had hypoglycemia. He suffered from very low blood sugar and needed to eat regularly. When Richard's blood sugar fell, he became anxious and moody, short-tempered and irritable. He also lost the ability to concentrate. Bill and Richard had worked out a plan whereby Richard would bring snacks to class and eat them whenever needed.

One day in the following March, Bill was absent from school because of an illness. A substitute took his place. During the lesson, Richard withdrew a sandwich from his backpack. The substitute, having no idea of Richard's condition, told him to put the sandwich away. Richard, believing that he had permission to eat in class, continued to munch away. The substitute seized the sandwich and threw it into the trash. Richard punched the teacher and was removed from the school by the police in handcuffs.

It was a situation that begged to be replayed. If only Bill had thought to tell the substitute about Richard's hypoglycemia. And so for Bill, the process of learning was activated by claiming some aspect of the sorrow as his own.

Deep learning can be the product of internalized responsibility—when we perceive how our actions led to a crisis or when we realize that the lesson failed because of our lack of planning. If we are able to attribute appropriately our sense of regret, then sorrow can be a source of learning and powerful future motivation.

REPRESSION, SUPPRESSION, AND COGNITIVE REFRAMING

In *Civilization and Its Discontents,* Freud (1930/1989) suggests that individuals are caught in a neurotic tug of war between their desires, passions, and emotions on one hand and the restrictions and restraints of living in a civilized community on the other. More recently, Barsade and Gibson (2007) write about our emotional reactions and our behavior in the workplace. They suggest that "the paradox we need to explore is that while authenticity may be desirable, regulation is essential to meeting personal and organizational goals" (p. 54).

Teachers find themselves in a similar dilemma. Most of us have experienced negative and potentially destructive emotions while teaching. If we are not going to act upon them, we must have choices in terms of how to deal with them. We can repress them by attempting to deny their existence. We hear this sometimes when a teacher may say, "I've never met a child I didn't like."

Alternatively, we can suppress them by trying to ignore their existence. We hear this when teachers say, "I am a professional. I'm not in the business of liking or disliking students."

Neither repression nor suppression are very satisfactory reactions. In either case, the emotional reaction is not being dealt with honestly. We suspect that when these negative emotions are not addressed, they can fester and create unhealthy stress associated with surface acting that can, in turn, lead to teacher cynicism and burnout.

An alternate strategy for dealing with negative emotions is to anticipate the emotions and engage in cognitive reframing. This is exactly what Diana did when she sought help from her principal in terms of her negative emotional reaction to the whiny girls in her fourth-grade class. She came to understand that the behavior of the girls clashed with her own feminist values and was able to move beyond her irritation in order to frame a goal for helping the girls to become more self-reliant.

Cognitive reframing involves creating the detachment necessary to entertain alternative perspectives, and this can be challenging to someone in the throes of an emotional flood state. However, in the long term, cognitive reframing causes much less stress than trying to regulate emotions through suppression or repression.

DETERMINING OUR DISPOSITIONS: SMILING BEFORE THANKSGIVING

To some extent, we can self-regulate our moods and dispositions by cognitive, emotional, and even *physiological* means.

Bill recalls his first year teaching at the special education school just outside of New York City. The students at the school were children and young adults with learning disabilities or emotional problems. Many of them had been expelled from public schools because of disciplinary problems, violence, or drug abuse. During his first few weeks at the school, a more experienced teaching colleague offered him the following advice for the classroom: *Don't smile until Thanksgiving, and don't laugh until Christmas!*

Bill's dour colleague misunderstood the relationship between class management and class climate. She assumed that any exhibition of playfulness or pleasantry early on in the school year would be interpreted by the students as a sign of weakness and would lead to classroom chaos.

Even more fundamentally, she failed to understand the bidirectional relationship between our emotions and physiology. It is common to assume that our facial expressions are a product of our emotions. So the theory is that we smile because we are happy or pleased, we scowl because we are angry, or we crinkle our brow as a result of some knotty problem or deep worry. However, research going back to the nineteenth century suggests that facial expressions are not only the external manifestations of emotions but that facial expressions have the power to provoke and produce emotional reactions in the people who express them. Darwin (1872) noticed that people who give way to violent gestures will actually increase their anger and rage. In 1890, William James wrote:

> There is no more valuable precept in moral education than this. . . . If we wish to conquer undesirable emotional tendencies in ourselves, we must assiduously, and in the first instance, cold bloodedly, go through the outward movements of those contrary dispositions which we prefer to cultivate. The reward of persistency will infallibly come, in the fading out of sullenness or depression, and the advent of real cheerfulness and kindliness in their stead. Smooth the brow, brighten the eye, contract the dorsal rather than the ventral aspect of the frame, and speak in a major key, pass the genial compliment, and your heart must be frigid indeed if it do not gradually thaw. (p. 198)

Bill discovered the bidirectional relationships between facial expressions and emotions by accident. Early in his career as a school administrator, he received feedback from teachers that he was not visible enough in and around the school. The message was clear, Bill needed to spend more time out and about the school and less time in the office. As a result, he decided to spend about twenty minutes each morning in the parking lot greeting the elementary children and their teachers as they arrived at school. After about a week of this practice, Bill realized that he was actually feeling more upbeat and cheerful as a result of these early morning sorties. He attributed this mood elevation to the fact that during the entire time he was greeting the children and their teachers, he was smiling. Researchers speculate that the act of smiling may release the neurotransmitter dopamine in the brain causing us to feel happier and more content.

Psychologists call this phenomenon *proprioception,* the fact that specific facial, vocal, and postural feedback patterns can actually produce corresponding emotions. In popular culture, perhaps Deborah Kerr best described this bidirectional relationship when she sang "I Whistle a Happy Tune" in the classic film *The King and I* (Lang, Brackett, & Zanuck, 1956, 1.1):

> Whenever I feel afraid
> I hold my head erect
> And whistle a happy tune
> So no one will suspect
> I'm afraid.
> While shivering in my shoes
> I strike a careless pose
> And whistle a happy tune
> And no one ever knows I'm afraid.
> The result of this deception
> Is very strange to tell
> For when I fool the people I fear
> I fool myself as well!
> I whistle a happy tune
> And ev'ry single time
> The happiness in the tune
> Convinces me that I'm not afraid.

In the song, Anna is not just disguising her fear from the outside world, she is actually transforming her inner emotional state by adjusting her posture, pose, and facial expression. She concludes that while she may have started out to deceive others, she ends up actually being able to reduce her own anxiety.

Hatfield, Cacioppo, and Rapson (1994) argue that the sight of a face that is happy, loving, angry, sad, or fearful can cause the observer to mimic the elements of that face and consequently catch the other's emotions. Paul Ekman (2003), probably the leading expert on facial expressions and their connections to emotions, goes even further. He suggests that when we "read" another's facial expression, we are not just processing information, but we are actually feeling the sensations that the other feels.

The social psychologist, Paula Niedenthal (Niedenthal, Krauth-Gruber, & Ric, 2006), conducted an artfully simple experiment that further illuminates the power of our own facial expressions in understanding the emotions of others. She asked two groups of participants to identify the emotional facial expressions of others. The participants in the experimental group were asked to clasp pencils in their mouths, thus severely restricting any facial movement. The other group had no such restriction. Niedenthal's hypothesis was that when we see an emotional facial expression, we automatically mimic it, and that mimicry actually helps us to understand the emotion of the other person. This was borne out in her experiment. The participants with the pencil clamped between their teeth (and so unable to mimic the emotional expressions they observed) were much less efficient in detecting the changes in emotional facial expressions than were the participants who were free to mimic the observed expressions.

CAN EMOTIONS BE OVERREGULATED?

In a word, yes. We have all met the stoic individual whose facial expressions offer very little clue to the emotions and feelings that may be present inside. Our reaction to the overcontrolled "mystery person" may range from vague awkwardness to downright suspicion and mistrust. People who lack affect in expression are not perceived as easily approachable. We simply can't read them. They are often seen as cold, distant, and aloof—certainly not the description of the personality that will forge strong supportive relationships with students.

To cultivate a classroom climate of trust, teachers must engage in a degree of *appropriate* self-disclosure. This does not mean that we need to share the details of a painful divorce or a struggle with drug dependency, but it might mean that we would share a meaningful reminiscence from our own childhood. We also need to share a degree of emotional openness.

Neither children nor adults will trust someone whom they do not know. Teachers must allow their students to know them. We must engage in self-disclosure and, at the same time, self-regulate our feelings.

The balance is to be strategic with our emotions.

**Activities, Exercises, and
Case Studies That Support
Teacher Emotional Self-Management**

PAUSING

Pausing comes to us from the work of Mary Budd Rowe (1987) on "wait time." She suggested that if teachers wait between three and five seconds after asking a higher-level question, three things tend to happen. First, students tend to respond in full sentences as opposed to single words and phrases. Second, reluctant participants tend to be more willing to contribute to class discussions (in some cases this may be children who process more slowly and need the extra time). And third, the level of deep critical and creative thinking increases dramatically.

Pausing in the classroom or in professional discussions slows down the number of frames per second of a conversation. It sends the important message: I am thinking about what you have just said. It also sends the message that thinking in this conversation is permissible and even encouraged. Neither of us are required to have prerehearsed or preconceived ideas. In the West, we often mistakenly equate the speed of a reply with intelligence. This is not the case in many non-Western cultures.

Pausing is an emotionally intelligent behavior in that it serves as a powerful preventative to personalized conflict. When we recall a conflict experience, we will often perceive an escalation of the speed of the inter-action. Person A says something. Person B responds instantly. Person A responds so quickly as to interrupt Person B, and so on, until someone regrets something that is said or words are misinterpreted by the other. Pausing prevents the escalation of rapidity.

PERSPECTIVE TAKING:
PRESUMING POSITIVE INTENTIONS

Directions: In each of the following vignettes, you will find yourself faced with an emotional challenge. The questions at the end of the vignettes ask you about the strategies you might use to stay "centered," take different perspectives, and manage your emotions.

"What's the point?"

Gabriel Millstream sits in the back row of the classroom. Since the start of the period, you've noticed that he seems somewhat irritable and distractible. Each time you have made eye contact with him, he has averted his eyes. You don't know Gabriel well since he has just been transferred into your class. The transfer was effected by the principal who gave a cryptic reason—something to the effect that there was a personality conflict between Gabe and his previous teacher. Another problem kid, you think to yourself. Just what I needed!

You finish an explanation of quadratic equations. The smart board is covered with examples and annotations. You pause and ask the class for their questions. Sarina in the front row raises her hand, but before you can call on her, Gabriel is on his feet. "What's the point of quadratic questions?" he demands. "Why are we wasting our time with this stuff?"

Discussion Questions

1. What are your initial thoughts about Gabriel's motivation for the question? What other intentions might he have?

2. How does Gabriel's question fit or fail to fit into your vision of the classroom decorum?

3. How might other students view Gabriel's question and your various responses to it?

4. What might be some emotionally intelligent ways to respond to Gabriel?

"How boring are you?"

Mr. Ian Johansen sits opposite you across the desk. You have just invited him to sit down, but you can tell that it is going to be a difficult parent conference. He did not shake your hand, and his lips are drawn thin against his teeth.

"Now," he begins, "I'll come straight to the point. My son, Harold, is in your class. You do know that don't you?"

You nod and open your mouth to reply, but Mr. Johansen cuts you off.

"No need to reply to rhetorical questions. Of course you know that Harold's in your class. But what you may not know is that he is bored out of his skull. I am not exaggerating. There is nothing about your class that he finds stimulating or challenging. Back in Plano, Texas, he was in a gifted and talented program. Those teachers understood how bright he is. But at this school, he's just treading water!"

Discussion Questions

1. What emotions does Mr. Johansen's complaint conjure up in you? How might these emotions be obstacles to a productive conference? How might you deal with these emotions?

2. How might you paraphrase Mr. Johansen's concerns in a way that presumes positive intentions on his part?

3. What might be an emotionally intelligent outcome for this parent conference?

"Branson's Retreat"

Branson Seagrave stands in front of you. He is dressed as usual in a dirty T-shirt and jeans—the waist band of which rests somewhere mid-buttocks. His hair is uncombed, and he sports a thick silver chain around his neck—from which hangs a black scorpion in an acrylic bulb.

It is the fourth time that Branson has failed to turn in his homework, and you believe it is time for a serious talk with him.

"You didn't turn in your homework," you say and wait for his reaction. Branson curls his lip into a sneer and shrugs.

"Did you do it?" you ask.

Branson's shrugs again and stares at his trainers.

"Why are you not doing your homework?" you ask. "Answer me!"

"I dunno." Branson mumbles.

"What do you mean 'you don't know'?"

"I dunno. Maybe I forgot or sumpthin'."

"Branson, I am tired of your attitude . . ."

At this point, tears well up in Branson's eyes; he turns on his heels and storms out of the classroom.

Discussion Questions

1. What emotions did Branson's reaction conjure in you? What are some ways to manage these emotions?

2. Looking back on the scenario, what are some other questions that the teacher might have asked Branson?

3. What is an emotionally intelligent way forward?

ROLE PLAY

Situation

Mr. Barrington and Mrs. Fairweather are sharing a classroom. Mr. Barrington is a traditional teacher who does a considerable amount of lecturing. He likes the classroom furniture set up in rows so that all the students face the whiteboard. Mrs. Fairweather, on the other hand, likes to use cooperative teaching groups and she moves the furniture to this end. She often forgets to move the desks back into rows at the end of her lessons. This infuriates Mr. Barrington. At first, Mr. Barrington attempted to make his unhappiness known through an e-mail to Mrs. Fairweather, but she responded with a critique of his "outdated" and "ineffective" instructional pedagogy. Mr. Barrington and Mrs. Fairweather have not spoken in more than a week. Yesterday, Mrs. Fairweather forgot to return the desks into rows, and Mr. Barrington's irritation spilled onto the whiteboard. He wrote in bold capital letters for all to see: THE CHAOS OF YOUR CLASSROOM IS A DISGRACE TO THE PROFESSION OF TEACHING.

Both Mrs. Fairweather and Mr. Barrington have now complained about the other to the principal. The principal has called a meeting to resolve the issue. This is that meeting.

One participant plays the role of Mrs. Fairweather, another Mr. Barrington, and a third the principal. There should be at least one process observer who watches for different emotions, how the characters manage them, and the strategies that the principal uses to move toward resolution.

CASE STUDY

Directions: Please read the case study below and address the discussion questions.

"Streamlining the Discussion"

The department meeting hadn't started yet. Holding a cup of steaming black coffee, Craig Watson fluttered around the coffee machine. His long pointed nose dipped periodically into the cup. He was like one of those toy birds—the ones that swing back and forth for hours dipping their beaks into a glass of water.

Craig Watson watched who was going to sit where.

Myra had positioned herself nearest to the door and was busy exhibiting the contents of a large plastic box. The scene could have been from a raid on a terrorist cell with the police laying out captured weaponry for newspapers to photograph. But here the grenades, rocket launchers, and assault rifles were replaced by pieces of fried bean curd, sharpened carrot and celery sticks, and miniature bludgeons of broccoli.

"Healthy food is so important for effective meetings. I think it takes the edge off people's tempers," Myra announced as she uncovered a bowl of blue cheese dip that smelled as though it were the grand prize in a sea-sickness competition.

Lilly Mayhall entered and seated herself at the head of the table. In his mind's ear, Craig could hear the drumroll of approaching royalty.

"My watch has three o'clock sharp. Shall we start?" Lilly phrased it as a question, but everyone recognized it as a statement of intention. Lilly Mayhall was the chairperson of the English Department.

Derek Blumberg and Craig Watson took seats as far as possible from the blue cheese dip. Wendy Williams drew up a chair next to Myra.

"The first item of business is the selection of the short stories for the ninth-grade unit. In order to streamline our discussion, I've made a list of stories I consider appropriate." Lilly distributed copies of the list to the other English teachers.

"How thoughtful of you," Wendy Williams commented. Craig listened for sarcasm, but failed to hear any. Myra started the fried bean curd and blue cheese dip around the table.

"Your experience is so valuable," Myra added, starting the broccoli bludgeons in a counterclockwise rotation around the table.

"Of course, nothing is set in stone. The input of professional colleagues is always valued. Comments?"

"There are some great stories on this list, Lilly," Derek spoke tentatively. "Hardy and Joyce are always great choices, but I wonder if our ESL students will find them accessible?"

"What do you think, Craig?" Lilly asked. "You have read the stories on the list, haven't you?"

Craig had just deposited a broccoli bludgeon in his mouth and had some difficulty responding. Finally he swallowed the broccoli floret whole and blurted out: "We do seem to have inherited quite a number of ESL students."

"I'm sorry. Perhaps I have misunderstood." Lilly began in a tone that clearly indicated that the chances of her misunderstanding were roughly the same as the survival of a frozen popsicle in a forest fire. "I thought the only students in the regular ninth-grade English classes were those who had graduated from ESL at the end of the eighth grade?"

Craig and Derek nodded.

"So you don't actually have any bona fide ESL students in your classes." The blue cheese dip arrived between Craig and Derek.

"Not in so many words," Derek agreed. "But the level of English among the recent ESL graduates is pretty low."

"Are these students not ready for mainstream English?" Lilly asked. "Have our brothers and sisters in the ESL department not been doing their jobs properly?"

"My gawd! What on earth is this?" Derek demanded, pushing the cheese dip as far as possible away from him.

"It's genuine Roquefort made from pasteurized sheep's milk!" Myra stared daggers at Derek.

"It smells like the crap I feed my roses!"

Craig attempted to refocus the team.

"It's not that they aren't ready for the mainstream," Craig murmured through masticated bean curd. "It's just the choice of materials. Maybe one size doesn't fit all."

"A clothing metaphor," Lilly grinned at Craig. "A little trite perhaps, but not nearly as crude as Derek's simile. But I'm afraid I don't agree," Lilly announced. "These students have two years in which to prepare for the International Baccalaureate program. We will be doing them an enormous disservice if we permit a watering down of the curriculum. Rigor, Mr. Watson, academic rigor is the mainstay of this department. Don't you agree, Derek?"

"Yes, of course. I wouldn't want to see a watering down of the . . ."

"Good. Our principal and the board of directors certainly don't want to see a fall in our examination results. Now, the next item on the agenda . . ."

Discussion Questions

1. What are some of the differing expectations that the characters have brought to the meeting? How do these expectations affect the outcome?

2. How do the characters manage or fail to manage their emotions?

3. What behaviors inhibit collaboration?

5 What Makes Us Tick

Teacher Motivation

Consider the following scenario: A fifth-grade student in the back of the classroom raises her hand. She waits patiently for the teacher to recognize and call upon her to speak. She then asks: "Why are you a teacher?"

How does the teacher respond? We suspect that the teacher's response may be predicated upon which words in the question the child selects to stress. If the child emphasizes *you*, the teacher may interpret the question as a thinly veiled impertinence and may respond defensively. If the child stresses some of the other words, the response may be very different.

Nevertheless, the question represents the elephant in the classroom that few teachers address explicitly. What is motivating the teacher? Why teach? Why not sell real estate or repair air conditioners? What on earth possesses someone to teach?

In this chapter, we will identify some of the sources of teacher motivation. We also debunk some commonly held myths about what actually motivates teachers. We will explore different educational belief systems and how working within our cognitive style can serve to motivate us. Finally, we will examine how teachers' dispositions and their sense of mission come together in motivation.

In recent years, the teaching profession in the West has been the victim of a great deal of criticism and not a little derision. Some of the criticism has been valid. The derision, on the other hand, has been destructive. Public ridicule always is.

Why would anyone enter a profession that has been heavily criticized and widely ridiculed?

What are some possible responses to our fifth grader's question? We might hear a teacher explain the need for employment. The teacher is performing a job in order to be paid a salary. In some cases, the teacher may cite content motivation—a passion for literature or science. In this case, the teacher may believe that content-area learning is important and will benefit students in the future. In other cases, teachers may identify relationship motivation and may explain how they love to work with children. Or they may assert that they are motivated by service to young people. Such service to others may give meaning to their lives. Such teachers may describe how they hope that the values they are instilling in children will produce a kinder and more humane world. Obviously, teachers are not pure types and most of us are motivated by numerous factors. However, much more than our cognition, it is our emotions that create and sustain our work motivation. Emotionally intelligent teachers tend to be highly self-motivated.

THE ROAD UP AND THE ROAD DOWN

Nearly two thousand years ago, Heraclitus (as cited in Hippolytus, c200, *Refutation*, 9.10.3) wrote that the road up and the road down are the same road. This may have some interesting geographical and philosophical implications, but it is not necessarily the case when it comes to the factors that motivate teachers.

More than twenty years ago, Fredrick Herzberg (1987) demonstrated that what satisfies and motivates us in the workplace are not the same things that dissatisfy and demotivate us. The road up and the road down are not the same road.

Herzberg attended City University in New York but left partway through his studies to enlist in the army. World War II was in full swing, and as a patrol sergeant, Herzberg was a firsthand witness to the liberation of Dachau concentration camp. He believed that this experience, as well as the talks he had with Germans living in the area around the camp, was what triggered his interest in motivation.

In 1959, Herzberg proposed the motivation-hygiene theory of job satisfaction. According to his theory, people are influenced by two factors: motivating factors and so-called hygiene factors. As the name suggests, motivating factors actually provide for work satisfaction and include achievement, recognition, the work itself, a sense of responsibility, promotion, and personal and professional growth. Each of these has a strong connection to our emotions. Professional satisfaction for teachers is an emotional reaction.

Hygiene factors, on the other hand, do not have the power to produce work satisfaction, but when they negatively influence the workplace, they can certainly foster dissatisfaction. Herzberg's hygiene factors include pay and benefits, company policy and administration, relationships with coworkers, physical environment, supervision, status, job security, and salary. In schools, like other workplaces, people are made dissatisfied by a bad environment, but they are seldom made satisfied by a good environment. However, Herzberg was quick to point out that the prevention of dissatisfaction was just as important as the encouragement of motivator satisfaction.

Hygiene factors operate independently from motivating factors. You can have highly motivated individuals who are also highly dissatisfied with their working conditions—take for example the idealistic peace corps' volunteer working in an impoverished, poorly equipped school in a developing nation in return for a pittance of a salary.

The truly counterintuitive connection here is between salary and professional satisfaction. The popular imagination suggests that a generous salary and benefit package will motivate teachers. Politicians are particularly fond of this simplistic formula. However, Herzberg found no linkage. He perceived salary as a hygiene factor. If the compensation was too low, it could and would dissatisfy, but large salaries were not associated with professional motivation or with high staff morale. In fact, some of the worst teacher morale can be found in some of the highest paid schools—no one can afford to leave. We have probably all experienced the short-lived euphoria associated with an increase in salary and have then soon come to take the increase entirely for granted—such is the nature of a hygiene factor.

This brings us to the issue of whether teachers are motivated by merit pay, bonuses, or other financial incentives. In our experience, such extrinsic rewards simply do not work in schools. Teachers, at least the ones we would want to work with, have gone into education because they are intrinsically motivated to make a difference in children's lives. Extrinsic rewards for such teachers may actually serve to reduce intrinsic motivation. We are motived by our values, and these are reflected in various educational belief systems.

EDUCATIONAL BELIEF SYSTEMS

Our preferred educational belief system(s) play a powerful role in our motivation and in determining our professional behavior. Accordingly, it is important for us to recognize and identify the values and beliefs that drive our emotions.

Let's take a moment and explore five different educational belief systems and how they may be motivating us and influencing our behavior: (1) academic rationalist, (2) self-actualizer, (3) cognitive processor, (4) technologist, and (5) social reconstructionist. This work is adapted from *Cognitive Coaching: A Foundation for Renaissance Schools* by Art Costa and Bob Garmston (2002).

1. Academic Rationalist

The academic rationalist sees the purpose of education to be the transmission of cultural heritage, basic knowledge, skills, and academic concepts from one generation to the next. If you have a preference for academic rationalism, you believe that there is a corpus of essential knowledge that a well-educated young person needs to master. You believe that there is great knowledge, truth, and wisdom to be found in the great thinkers of the past (e.g., "all philosophy is a footnote to Plato") and may advocate for a "liberal" education in which the cultural traditions of the past liberate young people from the fetters of contemporary myopia and prejudices.

You are motivated by high academic standards. Your preferred curriculum includes the classics and great books. You are concerned about the watering down of the curriculum and grade inflation. You are also concerned that the current move toward interdisciplinarity will reduce the depth and rigor of instruction. Your preferred teaching methodologies include lecture, note taking, demonstration, seminar, memorization, and drill. You are concerned that educational "fads" will diminish scholarship and academic standards. You are more concerned with content than with process.

You believe student assessment can be effectively carried out through summative examinations, achievement and standardized testing, and content mastery.

2. Self-Actualizer

If your preferred educational belief system is that of a self-actualizer, you have an orientation toward Gestalt and humanistic psychology. You perceive the purpose of education as the nurturing of each child's unique individual potential. Each child needs to be encouraged to develop personal integrity, a love of learning, creativity and sensitivity, and self-fulfillment. You believe that schools should be child centered with an explicit emphasis on student choice, democracy, and a classroom climate for learning and caring. Your perception of childhood may be through a Rousseauian lens.

Your preferred teaching style includes multisensory instruction (auditory, visual, kinesthetic, and tactual). You like to use learning centers, thematic approaches, and individualized instruction.

You are motivated by the idea that every student is capable of success. You believe that a trusting atmosphere is essential to a productive classroom. Student assessment should focus on growth in self-esteem and learning autonomy. You value student independence and self-direction. You may have been influenced by Abraham Maslow, Carl Rogers, Sidney Simon, and George Leonard.

3. Cognitive Processor

If you have a preference for the orientation of the cognitive processor, you believe that the primary functions of education are to develop clarity of thought in students, to use intellectual reasoning—particularly higher-level thinking skills—to solve complex problems and make rational decisions. For you, the goal of education is to assist students to learn how to learn. Your emphasis is on cognitive processes, metacognition, and problem solving.

You believe students need to be assessed by having them apply their knowledge and skills in real problem-solving situations. You prefer authentic performance tasks that are relevant to a student's real-world experience. You often use an inquiry-based approach and the Socratic method. You believe understanding is more important than content coverage.

You believe that students construct meaning by scaffolding new data to preexisting knowledge. Teachers mediate and facilitate that process by assisting students to see relevance and supporting them in making intellectual connections.

4. Technologist

The technologist is heavily influenced by behavioral psychology and the work of B. F. Skinner. If you have a preference for this belief system, you hold that learning can be measured through behavior. You have little time for aspects of education that cannot be measured, and you place a premium on quantifiable progress toward a clearly defined objective. You place an emphasis on the diagnosis of specific learner needs and abilities. You design instructional strategies that will develop skills and academic competencies. You see the purpose of education as producing young people who will function effectively in an ever-changing, complex technological society.

Your preferred teaching strategies include task analysis, the use of computers and learning systems with opportunities to diagnose the entry levels of students so as to determine what is known and what is yet to be learned.

You set clear and measurable objectives for yourself and your students within a reasonable time frame. You pay great attention to detail and hold that successful teaching depends on careful analysis, projection, and planning. You see education as a science. Learning can be planned and measured, and schools can be held accountable.

5. Social Reconstructionist

As a social reconstructionist, you are motivated by a belief that education can make the world a better place. You agree with H. G. Wells (1920) when he wrote, "Human history becomes more and more a race between education and catastrophe" (p. 4). You are oriented toward social justice and environmental protection. You care profoundly about social issues such as equal opportunity for minority groups and the peaceful resolution of conflicts. You believe that education can assist young people achieve a future condition of peace, a new world order based on equality of race, ethnicity, and gender. In education, you see the possibility of lasting solutions to war, overpopulation, racism, and the destruction of the environment. You see schools as the agents of positive social change wherein students are provided with opportunities to wrestle with social injustices, global and environmental issues, and the present problems of society. You agree with Kurt Hahn (as cited in Hellison, 2003) that the purpose of education should be to "make the brave gentle and the gentle brave" (p. 33).

Your preferred teaching methods include cooperative learning, simulations, role play, and outdoor learning pursuits. You want the students to develop social concerns and engage in activities such as community service. Your teaching resources include newspapers, current events, and present school problems.

You are highly motivated by the idea that education has a responsibility for bringing about a better, more humane future. You may have been influenced by Kurt Hahn, Paolo Freire, and Ivan Illich.

At the end of this chapter, there is a short quiz that you can take to determine your educational belief system preferences.

POLARITIES AND INTEGRATION

Each of the educational belief systems described above contains positive and constructive elements that do much to support effective learning for children. They can be perceived as polarities and, as such, can be a source of conflict. When governments, educational systems, or schools get into trouble, it is often because they have embraced one educational belief system at the expense of all the others. Such polarity may be politically expedient, but it is educationally simplistic and counterproductive. Many American educators would argue that the technologist approach of the No Child Left Behind Act of 2001 (with its obsession with objective accountability) caused many other important educational values to be neglected. Others might agree that the overemphasis of social reconstruction in Cuban education has caused critical and creative thinking skills to be ignored. Emotionally intelligent educators integrate their belief systems.

HOW WE WORK ALSO MOTIVATES US

Often when we think about what motivates us to teach, we think about the "what" of education: the content of our course or the larger goals and outcomes of our work. However, another motivating factor is our preference for how we actually go about our work.

Here we draw upon the work of Herman Witkin (Witkin, Goodenough, & Coc, 1975) and his theory of field-dependent and field-independent individuals. During World War II, the U.S. Air Force noticed that when pilots went into a spin, some pilots could right their planes without reference to the horizon; others needed external references in order to pull themselves out of the spin. The U.S. Air Force asked Witkin to examine this phenomenon, and his research developed into a theory of how styles of behavior, characteristics, and certain mannerisms indicate underlying psychological frames of reference. What began as a study of why some pilots could right their planes without external cues developed into a theory of cognitive style with more than fifty years of research. When we are working within our style preferences, the *way* in which we work can actually motivate us. When we are compelled to work far outside our style preferences, we can find ourselves demotivated.

All of us are some style combination of field independent and field dependent. There is some controversy about whether these styles can or do change over time. The original research suggests that these style preferences become fixed by about the age of five. However, our experience suggests that, at least to some degree, the styles are malleable. Most noticeably, we have witnessed school leaders move from the extremes of field independence and field dependence to a more balanced way of addressing work.

At the end of this chapter there is a brief style inventory that will give readers a window into whether they prefer field independence or field dependence.

Field Independence

The field-independent individuals often prefer to work alone and can be highly task oriented. They will get on with the job no matter what other people are doing. They can be competitive and enjoy recognition for individual accomplishment. Field-independent people often create a daily list of things to do and receive satisfaction from crossing things off that list. They will do their own thing regardless of what other people may think. They like to be the authors of their own goals and approach complex tasks by logical analysis and problem solving. They may not be very demonstrative of emotion and may not openly express affection for other people. Field-independent people like to figure out new things on their own, without help from other people. They enjoy working with abstractions and finding connections between unfamiliar concepts and their personal life.

Field Dependence

Field-dependent people need to perceive the larger context (the field) to make meaning out of a situation. They tend to be whole-to-part learners. They like to work in collaborative groups and teams, sharing responsibility and accountability. They enjoy team effort and thrive on synergy. They are highly motivated to help other people and often do not enjoy competitive activities. Field-dependent people are very influenced by what other people think. At best, they are socially sensitive and politically astute; at worst, they can be subject to peer pressure and paralyzed by empathy. They are very aware of other people around them and will interrupt their work to tend to the needs of others. They like to know exactly what is expected before they take on new responsibility. They also tend to be intuitive decision makers. They trust in their instincts and visceral responses. Field-dependent individuals are emotionally expressive and can be demonstrative in their affection for others.

There is no connection between cognitive style and intelligence. One is no better or worse than the other. However, when the expectations of the workplace and the responsibilities of the position match our style preferences, we can find both motivation and professional satisfaction.

PROFESSIONAL DISSATISFACTION: WHY DO THE WHINERS STAY FOREVER?

Why do the chronic complainers never seem to leave? Judge (1993; Judge, Thoresen, Bono, & Patton, 2001) and his research colleagues studied people who had positive dispositions but who were dissatisfied with their current jobs. They found that these individuals were *more* likely to leave their employment than dissatisfied employees with negative dispositions. They speculate that this may be because these individuals feel a higher degree of self-efficacy and believe in their ability to find another, more satisfying job. This may explain why the moaners never seem to leave on their own accord.

TEACHER DISPOSITION: MISSION AND MOTIVATION

Emotionally intelligent teachers have internalized motivation. They are self-directed and self-motivated. They are committed, and their goals are aligned with the objectives of the schools. They are willing to make personal sacrifices to help meet the larger goals of their students. These are individuals who contribute their time and energy to extracurricular activities with little or no extra compensation. These are individuals who use the school's core values in their professional decision making and find a sense of purpose in the school's mission.

Having a positive attitude is not just about being pleasant or convivial. Optimism and efficacy in teachers create team synergy and greatly enhance critical thinking and complex decision making. Amabile, Barsade, Mueller, & Staw (2005) found a strong linear relationship between greater positive mood and creativity in organizations. Researchers have also found that employees who experience positive moods at work are more likely to be motivated to engage in pro-social behavior both in terms of what their job requires and aspects that go beyond their job descriptions (George, 1991). Pro-social behaviors are those undertaken voluntarily to benefit or help another individual, group, or organization. Self-motivated teachers are much more likely to be engaged in providing students with extra help after school, leading afterschool activities, and involving themselves in community service projects.

Self-directed and self-motivated teachers take the initiative. They recognize and seek out opportunities, pursue goals beyond what is expected of them, cut through red tape and bend the rules when necessary to get the job done, and inspire others to mutual endeavor.

Self-motivated teachers have achievement drive. They constantly strive to improve their craft and precision as educators. They are results-oriented. They set challenging goals and take responsible risks. They accept uncertainty and ambiguity.

Self-motivated teachers are optimistic and hopeful. They persevere in the face of adversity and are able to set aside the fear of failure. They use setbacks as chances to learn and perceive crises and conflicts as opportunities.

Emotionally intelligent teachers combine positive disposition, motivation, and mission.

Activities, Exercises, and Case Studies That Focus on Teacher Motivation

EDUCATIONAL BELIEF SYSTEMS INVENTORY

We would invite you to take a short quiz that may help you identify which educational belief system(s) are influential in motivating your work as a teacher.

Directions: For each of the statements below, rank the sentence completions from 5 through 1 to reflect your personal educational values. Place 5 next to the statement that is *closest* to your value preference. Then, select the second-closest sentence completion and place 4 next to it, and so on. (Number 1 will be placed next to the sentence completion that *least* reflects your personal educational values.)

Next, insert the numerical response to each sentence completion in the scoring diagram (Figure 5.1) that follows the quiz. Add up each column, and then graph the totals on the pentagon. You should end up with something that looks like a lopsided star. The longest points of the star are your preferred educational belief systems.

1. The most important purpose of education is to

    A ____ assist students to learn how to learn.

    B ____ nurture the individual child's unique potential.

    C ____ produce trained young people who can function successfully in our ever-changing, complex technological society.

    D ____ inculcate traditions and values necessary for students to become constructive members of society.

    E ____ foster a new global society in which men and women can live in peace.

2. The most important job of the school is to

    A ____ foster wisdom through the rigorous study of history, literature, the sciences, mathematics, and so forth.

    B ____ provide students with the knowledge and values necessary to resolve social injustice and problems of society.

    C ____ help students to develop intellectual reasoning to solve problems.

D ____ cultivate a love of learning and self-fulfillment.

E ____ design effective instructional strategies that develop student academic skills and competencies.

3. The primary responsibility of the teacher is to

A ____ assist students in forming a global society based on mutual respect and equality of race, ethnicity, and gender.

B ____ diagnose learners' needs and abilities and establish measurable learning objectives.

C ____ allow full development of the student's creativity and sensitivity.

D ____ transmit to young people basic knowledge, skills, and academic concepts.

E ____ develop in students clarity of thought and precision in communication.

4. The most important educational outcome for students is to

A ____ develop personal integrity and self-fulfillment.

B ____ become intellectually discerning, rational decision makers.

C ____ become responsible global citizens.

D ____ understand the heritage and values of the past in order to walk boldly and wisely into the future.

E ____ become skillful in reading, writing, speaking, and computing.

5. The best instructional methods include

A ____ problem solving, Socratic method, and inquiry.

B ____ computers and learning systems with opportunities to diagnose student entry levels and prescribe according to what is known and what is yet to be learned.

C ____ demonstrations, lectures, seminars, memorization, and drill.

D ____ cooperative learning, simulations, role play, and outdoor learning pursuits.

E ____ multisensory instruction, student choice, self-directed learning on the part of the student, and individualized instruction.

6. In an outstanding school, emphasis must be placed upon

   A ____ the future of our planet, peaceful coexistence, the threat of overpopulation, and the protection of the natural environment.

   B ____ scholarship, high academic standards, and intellectual rigor.

   C ____ time on task, skills mastery, quality assessment, and accountability.

   D ____ the whole child, choice, democracy, creativity, trust, and caring.

   E ____ cognitive processes, metacognition, and high-level critical thinking.

7. The best curriculum includes

   A ____ classical literature and great books.

   B ____ field trips, real-life situations, and community service.

   C ____ task analysis, outcome-based learning programs.

   D ____ learning centers, interdisciplinary studies, and thematic approaches.

   E ____ problem solving, higher-level thinking, and decision making.

8. Assessment of student achievement should be based upon

   A ____ mastery of skills and competencies, pre- and posttests.

   B ____ self-evaluation and demonstrations of increased learning autonomy.

   C ____ how well students perform in actual problem-solving situations, application of knowledge.

   D ____ summative examinations, achievement tests, and content mastery.

   E ____ student involvement in constructive social change, development of a social conscience, and empathy.

9. The best metaphor for education is

   A ____ an input–output system in which data and opportunities to learn skills are provided.

   B ____ nurturing every child's unique potential.

   C ____ information processing.

   D ____ an instrument for constructive social change.

   E ____ transmission of essential truths and values from one generation to the next.

10. Rank the following statements from 5 (most agree with) to 1 (least agree with):

A _____ "Human beings are meaning makers, and schools and teachers mediate those capacities."

B _____ "The primary purpose of education is to civilize—to free the individual from the fetters of provincialism and prejudice by coming to know the knowledge and the wisdom of the past."

C _____ "Education has a sacred responsibility to bring about a better, more humane future."

D _____ "Learning can and must be demonstrated and measured—schools must be accountable."

E _____ "Each child is different, and his or her full potential can be nurtured."

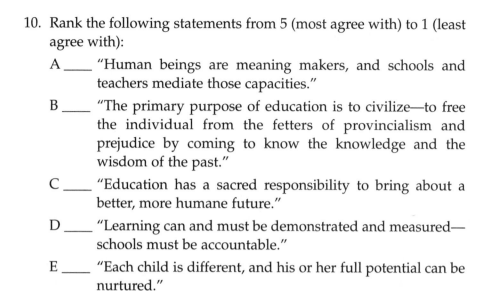

Figure 5.1 Scoring Diagram for Educational Belief Systems

Educational Belief Systems

Sentence Number	AR	SA	CP	T	SR
1	D =	B =	A =	C =	E =
2	A =	D =	C =	E =	B =
3	D =	C =	E =	B =	A =
4	D =	A =	B =	E =	C =
5	C =	E =	A =	B =	D =
6	B =	D =	E =	C =	A =
7	A =	D =	E =	C =	B =
8	D =	B =	C =	A =	E =
9	E =	B =	C =	A =	D =
10	B =	E =	A =	D =	C =
Totals					

(Continued)

Figure 5.1 (Continued)

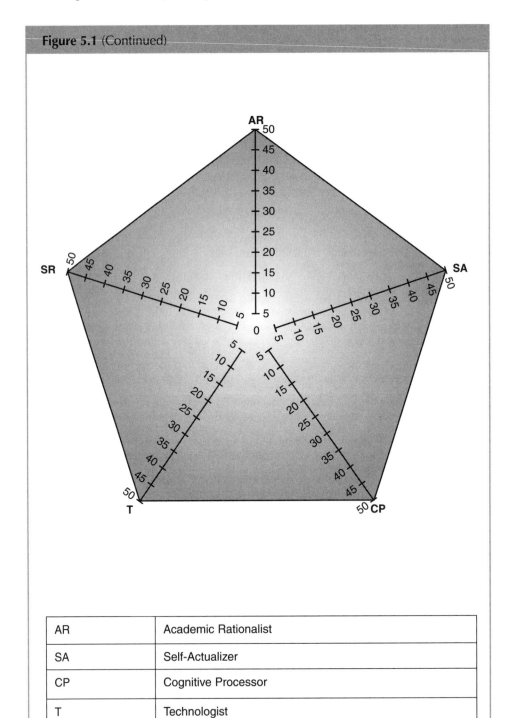

AR	Academic Rationalist
SA	Self-Actualizer
CP	Cognitive Processor
T	Technologist
SR	Social Reconstructionist

COGNITIVE STYLE INVENTORY

Directions: Put a check in the boxes below if the descriptor is like you. A check in the "2" box on the left-hand side indicates a strong similarity with the descriptor on the left-hand side of the page, a check in the "1" box a less strong similarity, and a "0" a balanced or neutral response. The checks on the right-hand side reflect a similarity with the descriptors on the right-hand side. There should only be one check per line.

	2	1	0	1	2	
I openly express my emotions.						I am hesitant to express emotions.
I openly express affection for others.						I am not demonstrative in expressing affection.
I like to work in groups.						I prefer to work alone.
I am influenced by what other people think.						I make my own decisions regardless of what other people think.
I like to help other people. I take pleasure in their accomplishment.						I enjoy competition and a sense of personal achievement.
I want to know exactly what is expected of me before I accept a task.						I want to set my own goals, standards, and work schedule.
I rely on intuition and gut responses when making decisions.						I use logic and analysis to solve problems and make decisions.
I like to be shown how to do something before trying it independently.						I like to experiment with new things on my own.
I need concrete examples in order to make sense out of things.						I enjoy working with abstractions and finding new connections.
I am relationship oriented.						I am task oriented.
Total points per column						

Scoring: Total each column. If you accumulated more points on the left side of the center line, you have a preference for field dependence. If you accumulated more points on the right side of the center line, you have a preference for field independence.

CASE STUDY

Directions: Please read the case study below and address the discussion questions.

"The Renaissance by the End of the Semester"

"We said we would get to the Renaissance by the end of the semester!" Maryanne snapped. She was the team's taskmaster. Set an objective and you could count on Maryanne to keep it clearly in focus.

"Maryanne's right, but I have a problem just plowing ahead with content when we know that the kids aren't picking up the skills they need." Gill pulled her bifocals down to the end of her nose and crinkled her brow.

"*Some* of the kids aren't picking up the skills," Maryanne retorted. "There are some major concepts in the study of the Renaissance that the kids will need in high school."

"I'll go along with whatever the team decides is important. I just feel a little uncertain about the student's writing skills," Gill conceded. "Teaching writing isn't my strong suit, and sometimes I think I just expect that the kids will pick up good writing through osmosis. I mean do we *teach* writing or do we just *mark* it?"

There was a long silence as the other two teachers digested Gill's question.

"It sounds as if you'd like us to look critically at how we teach writing," Carl added.

"I was disappointed in the last bunch of essays," Gill admitted.

"But," Maryanne cut in, "is it right to hold the entire eighth grade back because a few students . . ."

"Let's look at the data." Carl suggested. The three of them had marked the last batch of essays collectively. He flipped through his mark book until he came to the page he was looking for. He ran his fingers down the column of marks. "Almost a third of the eighth grade can't write a thesis statement, more than half weren't able to construct a well-organized paragraph, and only 15 percent had recognizable conclusions. Maryanne, I think we have our work cut out for us."

Maryanne took the mark book from Carl's hands. She ran her eyes down the scores that had been taken directly from the writing rubric. It was hard to argue with the data. "I agree that the kids need more work on writing—particularly on organization. I just don't want us to fall behind in content. The kids will need to know something about the Renaissance in the ninth grade. I'd really like them to understand how ideas of people like Galileo and da Vinci challenged the worldview of their day."

"You want them to understand that sometimes it's necessary to challenge authority in order to make human progress," Carl suggested.

"Exactly!" Maryanne cried.

"Does it have to be an either-or situation?" Carl asked. "Couldn't we do both?"

"You mean use the Renaissance as the content for a unit on essay writing?" Maryanne was intrigued.

"Absolutely." Carl grinned. "Let's play to our strengths by combining our classes. Maryanne and Gill could focus on the content, and I could explicitly teach the kids how to organize their essays."

"Could I come into your class when you teach organization?" Gill asked.

"Of course."

"But we would need to mark the essays together," Gill added, "like we did last time. We could then compare to see if the specific instruction had improved the organization of their writing."

"What are we going to do with the kids who already know how to organize an essay?" Carl asked. "It seems a waste of time to put them through it again."

"You mean differentiation. I'd like to see those kids research some of the Renaissance artists," Maryanne said.

"We could give them a special project—a choice of who they want to study," Carl suggested.

"The research project could involve technology, maybe even something using multimedia," Gill added. "It could be an individual learning contract."

"We know multimedia is high interest for the kids," Carl added. "Why don't we do it for all the kids?"

"Hang on," Maryanne interjected. "I thought our focus was writing."

"You're right. We need to stay focused," Carl agreed. "I'll prepare a lesson plan on essay organization. We certainly don't need to do that by committee."

"I'll come up with a list of Renaissance artists and writers for them to choose from. Maybe I could think about a role-play activity. The kids would enjoy that. But what's the primary concept we'd be teaching?" Maryanne paused to think. There was silence in the room for a long period. "I'd like our students to understand what a *renaissance* means—how it affected the way we think about culture, religion, art, education, and even how we define ourselves as a species. Let me think about it. I'll come up with something."

The bell rang.

"Let's get our stuff together and meet again tomorrow," Carl announced.

Discussion Questions

1. What evidence do you see in the case study of various educational belief systems in action?

2. What do the characters do or say that might suggest field dependence or field independence?

3. What evidence do you see of emotionally intelligent behavior?

6 Peripheral Vision

Teacher Social Awareness

> *The possibility that empathy resides in parts of the brain so ancient that we share them with rats should give pause to anyone comparing politicians with those poor, underestimated creatures.*

> —Frans B. M. de Waal (n.d., para. 1)

We are now moving into the complex realm of social awareness—how we gather information about the intentions, feelings, and thoughts of others and how we make sense out of them so that we can function competently in a social setting. In this chapter, we will be examining the key role that empathy plays in social awareness and how teachers use three specific types of empathy in the classroom. We will be exploring how important it is for teachers to empathize with the ignorance of their students and to actively "step into the shoes of misunderstanding." We will examine how nonverbal behavior can influence our social awareness and conclude the chapter with the controversial suggestion that, as a species, we humans may have an instinct for altruism that highly effective teachers connect with when they inspire their students.

But first, let's start with a brief story about an emotionally intelligent teacher.

PAULINE AND THE RASCALS IN GRADE-EIGHT SPANISH

Pauline came into Bill's coaching session clearly frustrated. Her brow was creased, her cheeks were flushed, and her lips were drawn against her teeth. Soon after they began the conversation, Pauline launched into a barrage of criticism leveled squarely at her grade-eight Spanish class. Conscientious and highly organized, Pauline planned meticulously for every lesson. However, unlike the rest of her classes, the grade-eight Spanish group couldn't seem to stay focused, and Pauline was rarely able to finish her lesson plan. They were good kids but a bit "rascally." Pauline spoke anxiously of how she would consult her watch, realize that there wasn't going to be enough time to finish the lesson, and accelerate the pace of instruction.

Bill paraphrased her feelings of annoyance and asked how the grade-eight students reacted to the increased pace. Pauline threw up her hands. The acceleration seemed to produce even more disengagement on the part of the students. She described how annoyed she was that she would expend great effort and time in planning, only to receive such an apathetic reaction from her students. "I work incredibly hard for them, and they don't seem to care!" At one point, Pauline's eyes welled up with tears of frustration.

She went on to describe her vain attempts to hide her impatience and irritation from the students. "I don't want them to see me angry with them. I know that doesn't do any good." Quite suddenly, Pauline's facial expression changed. The mask of anxiousness and irritation faded and was replaced by an expression of calm puzzlement. She was silent for a long moment. "Maybe, maybe I'm trying to do too much. Do you think I'm overplanning?" she asked rhetorically. Pauline went on to question her planning process and the "tyranny" that her lesson plan held over her instructional performance. She began to wonder whether she needed greater flexibility. She recognized that her irritation was having a negative effect on the students, and she began exploring how she might attempt to avoid feeling such negative stress.

At the conclusion of the conversation, Pauline was determined to build at least ten minutes of what she called flextime into her ninety-minute lessons so that the end of the lesson could include enjoyable activities such as games, software applications, or other enrichment activities. During the conversation, Pauline had taken herself from a state of low efficacy in which she was blaming the students for apathy and laziness to a state of significantly increased resourcefulness in which she was planning how she could reduce her own stress and, she hoped, improve the social dynamic between herself and her students. She had accomplished an important perceptual shift. She had moved the focus of her thinking from herself and the goals of her teaching to an understanding and appreciation of what might have been going on for her students and their learning. She had become more flexible in her thinking, more socially aware, in short, more empathetic.

A week later, Bill had a second conversation with Pauline in which she reported a much-reduced personal stress level. The class, in her words, had been "transformed." The students were on task most of the time. An atmosphere of playfulness had begun to permeate her interaction with the students, and there was more laughter. She reported being pleased with the progress the students were making and confident of her work with them.

Social cognition is the processing of information that leads to accurate interpretations of the dispositions and intentions of others and self. This is no small challenge. Not only must we become self-aware—know our own attitudes, dispositions, and motives—but we must also be reasonably accurate in estimating them in others. So in order to be socially competent, we need to engage in a form of mind reading, not exactly telepathy but a close cousin as we see later in this chapter.

What does it mean to accurately interpret our dispositions and intentions? On the surface it sounds fairly simple and straightforward. However, in the dense thicket of our emotions, knowing our intentions can be both complex and demanding.

It was only after Pauline had clarified her intentions (student learning as opposed to getting through her lesson plan) that she was able to see how her frenetic behavior in the classroom might have been counterproductive.

THE ROAD THAT'S PAVED WITH GOOD INTENTIONS

As a general rule, many of us who teach do not spend much time clarifying our intentions. In the midst of our busy professional lives, we tend to assume that our motives need no examination, and therefore, we often rush headlong into planning strategies and behaviors that will help us realize our goals before knowing exactly whether the goals reflect the outcomes we truly desire. This is crucial to social cognition because our intentions are often linked to our deeply held values. And when those values are not clear or are in conflict with one another, we can easily journey down the proverbial path that is paved with good (but unexamined or confused) intentions.

For example, when a teaching colleague comes to us despairing of a class he is teaching, how do we respond? To a large extent, our response is determined by our intention. Do we respond as a friend and tell him that he has just had a bad day, that he's a great teacher and invite him out for a coffee? If we do so, our intention is to make the other person feel better and to preserve fellowship. Alternatively, we can respond as a consultant and offer him advice about how to handle his difficult class. If we determine that the consultant role is appropriate, then we choose to take on the mantle of the expert and suggest solutions. Our intention is to support a colleague in his effort to manage a class. Another response might be that of a supervisor. We might recommend some form of professional development. In this case, our intention might be quality and damage control. A different response might be that of a coach, in which we would paraphrase and probe in order to support the colleague's own thinking about his difficult class. In this last instance, our intention is to support the cognition and growth of the teacher concerned.

Each response may be appropriate or not. The critical issue is to determine our intention given the specific situation and then choose congruent behaviors. This is one of the basic capabilities in Cognitive Coaching.

Paying attention to intention is one of the foundations of healthy social cognition.

SOCIAL AWARENESS AND EMPATHY

Empathy is the key to social awareness. In a recent issue of *Educational Leadership* that focused on the theme "Reaching the Reluctant Learner," Landsman, Moore, and Simmons (2008) turned the tables and wrote an article on the relationship between "reluctant teachers" and "reluctant learners":

> Reluctant teachers often avoid students who do not look, act, or talk like them. They may categorize such students as being at risk, having behavior problems, or being unteachable. . . . Teachers who define students in such terms create a classroom environment that is no longer a place of learning and high expectations but rather a place rooted in control and management. Such conditions will not help the reluctant learner become successful. (p. 62)

We would suggest that such reluctant teachers suffer from a selective failure of empathy. Empathy allows teachers to sense what contributes to a class climate that is low in destructive anxiety and high in challenge (Willis, 2007). But empathy and social cognition develop at very different rates in different individuals. The frontal lobe, the area of the brain that is central to social cognition, develops slowly and doesn't reach full maturity until our late teens or early twenties. (In this area, girls tend to mature earlier than boys.) This means that a classroom will often represent an enormous range of social cognition—from extremely simple and concrete to complex and sophisticated empathy.

Studies suggest that the roots of empathy may extend back into early infancy. Campos and Sternberg (1981) reported that when very young children are placed in ambiguous situations, they will scan their parents' faces in order to "read" their emotional response—anger, surprise, happiness, or fear. Studies have shown that the facial expressions of parents can instill confidence or insecurity in young children and can have a determining effect on the infant's behavior.

There are three types of empathy that exist in the classroom. These are based upon the simulation theory that has emerged out of developmental psychology. The premise behind simulation theory (Gordon & Cruz, 2003) is that we do not intellectually analyze each new situation we find ourselves encountering. Instead, we come to understand other people's mental states by literally pretending to be in other people's shoes, simulating the emotional situation of the other person. There are two schools of simulation thought. The first is that we develop the pretense of being in the other's position by deliberate, cognitive effort. The alternate version suggests that we attend the simulation automatically in a virtually unconscious fashion.

When we examine the three types of empathy that are present in the classroom, we see examples of both automatic and deliberate simulation.

The first type is *primal empathy*. This is when we witness the suffering of another person and involuntarily feel some of the other person's pain. Primal emotional empathy is at work when we wince at the sight of a homeless person on a cold winter night or when we grimace at the sight of an athletic injury. Primal emotional empathy does not involve cognition or deliberation. We do not consciously think about the pain of the other person, we simply feel it. Our response is in the brain's limbic system. It is automatic, before thought.

The second type is *contextual empathy*. This is empathy for the situation or context that the other person is in. Contextual empathy requires cognition. We need to recognize the situation the other person is in, project ourselves into the other person's position, and imagine what he or she is feeling and thinking. With contextual empathy, previous experience and cultural background play an important role. For example, many Muslims have an aversion to dogs. They view canines as unclean animals, perhaps in a similar fashion to the way some people in the West view rodents. Thus, tying a red ribbon around the neck of a cute beagle puppy and presenting it to the local Imam on his birthday may send contradictory messages. If we do not understand the cultural influences acting upon the other person, we may be unable to understand the context of their situation, making empathy impossible.

The third type is *cognitive empathy*. This is when we attempt to understand the thinking of another person—when we actually try to get inside another person's head and understand their cognition. Cognitive empathy is what John Medina (2008) calls *theory of mind*. There are numerous strategies that teachers use for cognitive empathy, among them "making thinking visual" and "think aloud" techniques. One of the most challenging aspects of cognitive empathy for teachers is to recall what it was like for us *before* we became content-area experts, to empathize with the novice learner. Even more challenging is empathy that leads to the uncovering of student misunderstandings and misconceptions.

STEPPING INTO THE SHOES OF MISUNDERSTANDING

In our differentiation workshops for teachers, we use the analysis of student work as a vehicle for teachers to come to a deeper understanding of their students as learners. One strategy is to provide the workshop participants with twelve sample solutions to the same math problem. A couple of the solutions arrive at the correct answer and clearly explain their calculations. A number of the other attempts arrive at incorrect answers but suggest that the students may have understood the concept, even though they made arithmetic errors. Some of the samples involve highly unusual and creative solutions. The issue for the workshop participants is to attempt to get inside the thinking of these students. Once we can engage in cognitive empathy, we can determine what the students understand or are confused about. This allows us to plan the next steps of instruction meaningfully.

All three forms of empathy are important in the classroom, but cognitive empathy is critically important for further student learning; however, it can be a difficult process. How often have we asked students, "What is it about this topic that you don't understand?" And how often have we heard, "I don't know what I don't understand." This is almost certainly true but is not very helpful to the teacher who is trying to help a student understand algebra. The danger that experts confront is that we are so familiar with our subject that we forget what it is like to think like a novice. This ability to step into the shoes of misunderstanding and to recall our own stages of ignorance is part and parcel of the craft of cognitive empathy.

EMPATHY AND CRUELTY

The challenge of social awareness for teachers is great. They need acute and astute peripheral vision to take in the full social dynamics of the classroom. They need to recognize the pride of Melvin who has just been given the lead in the school play, the anxiety of Olga who believes that the physics course is too difficult for her, the frustration of Juan who has a learning disability and is reading three grade levels below the class, the pain of Myra whose boyfriend has just broken up with her, and so on.

Empathy builds upon self-awareness. The more we are aware of our own emotions, the greater the likelihood that we will recognize them in others and therefore extend ourselves to them. The degree to which a teacher is able to establish rapport with students is the degree to which there is emotional attunement. A class climate of caring is born and bred out of our capacity for empathy.

Cruelty has been defined as the failure of the imagination—the inability to empathize with the victim. This is true in many cases, particularly in reports from the perpetrators of racism and genocide. They failed to perceive their victims as fellow human beings. However, our capacity for deliberate, premeditated cruelty seems also to be borne out of a twisted sense of empathy—empathy that somehow detaches emotion, intellect, and conscience. In *Othello*, Shakespeare (1623/2004) creates a truly evil character in the shape of Iago. Iago deceives Othello into believing that his beloved Desdemona is having an affair with Cassio. Iago masterfully manipulates the situation so that Othello flies into a rage of mad jealousy, and the bloody tragedy unfolds. Iago may be devoid of conscience, but we would argue, he has considerable, albeit perverted, empathy. He understands how the other characters feel and think, and this allows him to manipulate them in the cruelest of fashions. He displays his skill at deceiving other characters so that not only do they not suspect him, but they count on him as the person most likely to be truthful and trustworthy!

Clearly our capacity for empathy varies from individual to individual. Some people are extremely empathetic even to the point of being "paralyzed" by it. This can be the case in school leaders who are reluctant to make difficult and unpleasant decisions about the contract renewal of ineffective, but likeable, teachers.

On the opposite end of the spectrum, there are some individuals who genuinely appear to have little or no empathy. Fortunately, they are few and far between. Psychologists refer to them as psychopaths. A short vignette illustrates the difference between mental cleverness and emotional intelligence.

THE ENDS JUSTIFY THE MEANS: A STORY OF A HIGH SCHOOL PSYCHOPATH

The first inkling that anything was wrong came when the high school principal and counselor sought an urgent, late afternoon appointment with

Bill, who at the time was the headmaster of the International School of Tanganyika (IST) in East Africa.

Both the principal and counselor were grim faced and tense.

Slowly the story emerged. For many years, Lafayette College had provided an outstanding graduate of IST with a full four-year scholarship. Several of the school's seniors had applied for it, including two friends of many years standing, we'll call them Ali Jaffer and Ted Muffort. Both were fine students who nurtured aspirations of going into engineering. However, Ali Jaffer was truly exceptional, and his teachers predicted that he might even get a perfect 45-point IB (International Baccalaureate) diploma. When the date for the scholarship application decision came and passed and nothing had been heard from Lafayette College, the counselor, who knew the director of admissions personally, called through on the phone.

The director of admissions expressed disappointment that Ali Jaffer had withdrawn his application since with his sterling transcript, glowing recommendations, and outstanding predicted exam results, he would have been a natural for the scholarship. It was the first that the counselor knew that Ali had withdrawn his application.

It was also the first that Ali knew about it. The counselor followed up, and the admissions director faxed through a copy of the letter of withdrawal. Needless to say, it was a forgery. The counselor then contacted all of the universities that Ali Jaffer had applied to. The story was the same. Both MIT and Georgia Tech had received similar withdrawal letters. The only university that Ali had applied to that hadn't received such a withdrawal letter was Stanford. The counselor put two and two together.

She had a conference with Ali, who refused to believe that his applications had been withdrawn. Ali actually produced an e-mail from MIT stating that his application was being processed.

Ted Muffort had applied to all of the same universities as Ali Jaffer except Stanford. The counselor contacted the admissions directors at MIT and Georgia Tech, and she reviewed Ted's application files with them. Ted's file in each case was a forgery. Ted's purported transcript and letters of reference were actually those written for Ali.

Bill and the high school principal confronted Ted. After a while, when it became apparent that lying was leading nowhere, Ted told the truth. He had broken into the counselor's office and made copies of Ali's file. He had then doctored Ali's transcript and letters of reference on his computer to appear that they had been written for him. He had e-mailed all of the universities in which he and Ali might be in competition for admission or scholarships, withdrawing Ali's applications. When several of the universities refused e-mail communication, Ted had followed up with hard-copy letters. Ted had even managed to hack into the MIT admissions' office computer and had sent Ali a fraudulent e-mail stating that his application was still in process.

When asked how he could bring himself to systematically sabotage his friend's university applications, Ted shrugged and said that he had wanted to gain entrance to a prestigious university to please his parents. Ted appeared to feel nothing for his "friend" and expressed no regret or remorse. He was sorry to have been caught and was upset that his own future career plans were in tatters. It appeared to Bill that Ted was unable to experience any empathy and so behaved in a way that was devoid of morality or any ethical considerations. Ted was unquestionably clever. However, his manipulative cunning only mimicked emotional intelligence. Like other perpetrators of evil, Ted was both pathetic and terrifying.

THE CHALLENGE OF EMPATHY

In his public speeches, His Holiness the Dalai Lama (Dalai Lama & Ekman, 2008) is fond of telling the story of a Tibetan monk who, following the Chinese invasion of Tibet, was held in a Chinese prison for a long time. After many years, the monk was released and escaped across the border to Dharamsala in India where he met with the Dalai Lama for many hours. During his conversation with the Dalai Lama, the monk mentioned that occasionally during his imprisonment he had experienced profound fear.

The Dalai Lama (Dalai Lama & Ekman, 2008) then asked the monk what kind of danger he had perceived. And the monk replied that he felt he was in danger of losing his compassion . . . for the Chinese prison guards.

Teachers are not often asked to face the empathetic challenge of the Tibetan monk; nevertheless, empathy is essential for their work with children and young adults. Empathy allows teachers compassion for their students. Compassion is not just feeling sorry for another person. It is momentarily entering their world and understanding their fears, their sufferings, insecurities, passions, and worries.

MINDSIGHT

Empathy allows us to develop what the psychologists call *mindsight*, the ability to "read" what may be going on in other people's minds. While this is not exactly telepathy, it is a vital skill that allows us to navigate social situations. Mindsight may have its genesis in our brutish prehistory when determining our neighbor's intentions could have been a matter of life and death. Mindsight requires that we recognize our separateness from other people (something that very young children may not be able to do), understand that people may think differently than we do, and be aware that other people may perceive situations differently and have intentions that may or may not be in our own best interest.

Children and adults who suffer from autism or Asperger's syndrome typically have very limited mindsight and find it extremely difficult to learn from social cues. They cannot read facial expressions and will often avoid eye contact. These children often need to be taught the components of social interaction through direct instruction. Temple Grandin is probably America's best-known person with autism. She was diagnosed with autism in childhood. Extremely bright, Grandin has authored a number of books and is a frequent conference speaker on the humane care of livestock. However, socially Grandin (1995) has great difficulty. She writes of using the automatic doors at the supermarket to gauge and practice establishing appropriate interpersonal space for interaction with other people.

EMPATHY AND INTUITION

Empathy works on a conscious and subconscious level. This is because the human brain can be likened to a filter.

We find filters in automobiles, coffee machines, and air conditioners. The job of the filter is to separate that which is passed through from that which is retained. The brain works in a similar fashion. We pay conscious attention to only a minute fraction of the sensory stimuli that bombard our brain every second. If the brain did not filter out almost all of this, we would be dysfunctionally overloaded. However, it is important to recognize that conscious processing is only a small portion of the processing that occurs in the brain. Most of what we do in terms of our brain activity is subconscious and "it is the exception, not the rule, when thinking is conscious; but by its very nature, conscious thought seems the only sort. It is not the only sort; it is the minority" (Lachman, Lachman, & Butterfield, 1979, p. 207).

In the same way, much of our processing of emotional information goes on subconsciously. We receive hints and clues of this subconscious processing through our dreams and what psychologists refer to as *somatovisceral* reactions—our intuitive or "gut" responses. In our somatovisceral responses we feel attracted or repulsed by something or someone, but we may be unable to consciously identify the reasons for this reaction. Hatfield (Hatfield, Cacioppo, & Rapson, 1994) calls the brain a *parallel processor* in that it works both rationally and intuitively. When we engage in a conversation with a colleague or a friend, we are listening and analyzing the content, but we are at the same time constantly monitoring our partner's emotional reactions. We do this both consciously and subconsciously by paying attention to a variety of subtle indicators: facial expressions, muscle movement, tone of voice, and the timing of the reaction.

While most facial expressions last for two or three seconds, some expressions last only a fraction of that: $\frac{1}{25}$ of a second. Ekman (2003) has undertaken extensive research in this field. He refers to these fleeting contractions of facial muscles as *microexpressions* and believes that they occur when people are deliberately concealing how they feel or when people have blocked from awareness (repressed) the emotions they are experiencing.

Ekman believes that our emotions are involuntarily registered in facial muscle contractions. He has identified seven emotions that are universal for all people irrespective of culture: anger, fear, sadness, disgust, contempt, surprise, and happiness. The so-called microexpressions are not something we can control, but they occur so quickly, in $\frac{1}{15}$ to $\frac{1}{25}$ of a second, that the observer may not consciously recognize them. However, we may recognize them on a subconscious level, which may produce a somatovisceral or intuitive reaction.

Ekman (n.d.) has devised an hour-long online training program that claims to substantially improve our ability to recognize these microexpressions and thus determine whether other people are telling the truth. The METT (Micro Expression Training Tool) program has been used to train U.S. government employees, law enforcement officers, medical professionals, and corporate executives from Fortune 500 companies (see www.paulekman.com).

A number of years ago, Bill was recruiting teachers for an international school in Africa. It was late in the recruitment season, and he was desperate for an experienced learning disabilities specialist. He interviewed a candidate in California who seemed perfect. She was well qualified, experienced, articulate, and intelligent. She had glowing references and seemed eager to work in Africa. But there was something wrong that Bill couldn't put his finger on. He lost sleep over the decision, but ultimately decided to "go with his gut." He did not hire the candidate and returned to school with the vacancy unfilled. A year later, he heard from an administrator at a different school who had hired the special education candidate that she had been a disaster. She had been extremely high emotional maintenance, had fought with colleagues and parents, generally lowered staff morale, and (to the relief of the administrator) had broken contract. Bill was never sure what caused warning bells to go off in his head about this particular candidate, but it may have been his subconscious reading of her microexpressions during the interview.

FEELING BEFORE KNOWING: AFFECTIVE BLINDSIGHT

Now we move into the realm of the weird and wonderful. There is some evidence that we experience emotional reactions *before* we are actually conscious of them. This may help explain what we commonly call intuition— something emotionally intelligent teachers use daily in the classroom.

Recent research with stroke patients has revealed some fascinating information about how the brain processes some emotional information and has revealed a condition that neuroscientists refer to as *affective blindsight* (de Gelder, Vroomen, Pourtois, & Weiskrantz, 1999). A middle-aged man suffered several strokes that destroyed all the connections between his eyes and the visual cortex of the brain. So, although his eyes could register images, his brain could not decipher them. Our stroke patient was, for all intents and purposes, blind.

When he was shown pictures of geometric shapes or even photographs of people, he had no idea of what he was looking at. However, when he was shown pictures containing overtly angry, fearful, or happy faces, he was able to guess the emotions expressed with an accuracy that far exceeded mere chance.

Researchers undertook to scan the stroke patient's brain while he was guessing the emotions represented in the pictures. These scans revealed an alternate passage for emotionally laden sensory information. Normally, the flow of visual stimuli goes from the eyes to the thalamus and then to the visual cortex. The alternate passage illustrated in our stroke patient (and operable in ourselves) sent the information straight from the thalamus to the amygdala (the amygdala is the portion of the brain that extracts emotional messages from nonverbal information). The nonverbal message might be another person's joyous grin, scowl of anger, or tremor of fear.

The incredible finding is that the amygdala extracts this emotional information milliseconds *before* we know what we are looking at!

The amygdala has no links to the brain's center for speech, so when we register an emotional reaction, we are often at a loss to understand or express why we may be feeling in such a way. And so the direct thalamus to amygdala emotional link may help to explain some of what we experience as intuition.

Intuition and empathy are a teacher's primary tools of social awareness in the classroom.

ESCAPING THE CELL OF SELF

Self-absorption kills empathy. The more focused we are on self, the less attention we pay to others and to the social world around us. Individuals who perceive themselves to be in positions of power and authority are particularly prone to self-absorption. This is especially the case when a teacher has a challenging class and may come to perceive the situation as a power struggle. Such self-absorption can take numerous forms—from externalizing responsibility for student failure ("Those kids should never have been placed in this class. I don't know what the counselor was thinking"); to presuming negative intentions on the part of students ("They just don't care."); to drawing conclusions that are even more dehumanizing ("You know the family background/culture these kids come from. They're hopeless").

We are less likely to experience self-absorption if our intention is student learning as opposed to class management and control. When our outcome is learning, empathy is a means to an end. When our goal is control, empathy is an obstacle.

Teacher empathy in the classroom doesn't rely just on verbal communication. Much of what we "read" about students comes from their nonverbal behavior, from their facial expressions, from their tone of voice, from their posture, and of course, from their gestures.

A GESTURE: WORTH A THOUSAND WORDS

How teachers read student gestures can give us insight into what they understand and misunderstand. Gesturing in children may even be *predictive* of future learning. Susan Goldin-Meadow (1997; Goldin-Meadow, Wagner Cook, & Mitchell, 2009) from the University of Chicago has studied the speech-gestures mismatches of young children (when the verbal language and the physical gestures are not congruent) and suggests that in such cases, the gestures may be harbingers of deeper and more sophisticated concept attainment.

Take, for example, Jean Piaget's classic experiment on concept development in young children. The researcher takes a tall, slender glassful of water and pours it into a broad but shallow dish. A young child observes the action and is then asked which dish contains the most water and to explain his or her answer. Researchers have noticed that when young children answer incorrectly that there is less water in the shallow dish because the water level in the tall glass is higher, the child's fingers may form a narrow figure C indicating the circumference of the tall glass and then a wider C when representing the shallow dish. While the child's words focus only on the height of the water level, the child's hands indicate a future understanding of the influence of the vessel's width. Iacoboni (2008) writes:

> Typically, though not always, gestures are "ahead" of speech in these childhood mismatches. . . . The gestures tend to convey the more advanced concepts. They facilitate learning. . . . Indeed, the mismatchers show a better ability to generalize recently acquired knowledge and concepts than the "skippers"—that is, kids who proceed from incorrect explanations matched in speech and gestures to correct explanations matched in speech and gestures. (p. 81)

Michael Grinder (1991) and others have done extensive work studying teachers' nonverbal communication in classrooms and have confirmed the powerful impact that gesturing and other nonverbal behavior can have on student learning. Children are extremely sensitive to the gestures of teachers. When teacher gestures and nonverbal behaviors match the concept under discussion, learning is enhanced. When there is a mismatch, learning is inhibited. For example, take the fifth-grade teacher who is introducing the concept of simple algebraic equations (say, $6 + 4 + 3 = 5 + ?$). If the teacher points to each item in sequence, the gesture coupled with the plus signs may lead the child to add the numbers and come to the incorrect conclusion that the question mark should be replaced by the number 18. However, if the teacher uses a "visual paragraph" to illustrate how each side of the equation is different but equal, perhaps even mimicking a balance scale with arms outstretched, the child is more likely to understand the concept of equations.

Posture is another nonverbal student response behavior that teachers can "read." One research study tracked the postural shifts of students in a classroom. The more similar their postures were to that of the teacher, the more strongly the students felt rapport and the greater their overall level of engagement in the lesson (LaFrance & Broadbent, 1976). In fact, this study suggests that posture matching may be a quick and surprisingly accurate way to gauge the climate or atmosphere of a classroom.

THE EMPATHY PARADOX

There is, however, an interesting paradox when it comes to how accurately people are able to self-assess their own empathy. Research (Davis & Kraus, 1997) suggests that there is *no* correlation between how accurate people think they are at reading other people's feelings and how the same person actually performs on objective tests of empathy. However when other people, who know the person well, evaluate the individual's empathy, there is a high degree of correlation with the test results. The irony may be that the more we become skilled at practicing empathy, the more we realize how deficient we are at it. The empathy paradox also highlights the fact that there are dimensions of self and our relationships in which other people may know us better than we know ourselves.

POWER, AUTHORITY, AND EMPATHY

There is also a political dimension to empathy that is worthy of a moment's reflection. Groups who have little political power (often including students, laborers who do menial work, or members of ethnic minorities) are expected to sense and understand the feelings of those who hold power and authority. More significantly, those who hold power, whether ascribed or informal, feel much *less* of an obligation to be sensitive or empathetic in return. Power and authority can actually desensitize us to less influential individuals and groups. Historically, the denial of empathy has been a key feature of those in power when asserting their control over other less fortunate groups and has been a foundational feature in racism and other forms of collective exploitation.

In the early 1960s, Martin Luther King Jr. spoke about his surprise at how little insight Caucasian Americans had into the feelings of African Americans. King asserted that African Americans had to be much more sensitized to how Caucasian Americans felt if only to survive in a racist society. Denial of empathy has been and continues to be one of the strongest subconscious forms of racism.

Elaine Hatfield (Hatfield et al., 1994), a psychologist at the University of Hawaii, has undertaken extensive research in the in the area of empathy. Her conclusions, included in her book *Emotional Contagion*, suggest a negative correlation between occupying a position of power and empathetic ability. This would strongly suggest that teachers who perceive their relationship with students as one of power and authority are likely to be far less empathetic than those who do not perceive power and control to be major dimensions of learning relationships.

An administrative colleague of ours never left an interview with a prospective teacher without asking her favorite question: "Can a teacher be *too* empathetic?" Prospective teachers who had reservations about their own empathy in the classroom were often teachers who lacked the skills necessary to establish constructive learning relationships with students. Empathetic teachers sense their students' feelings and perspectives and take an active interest in their concerns. They are attentive to emotional cues and listen actively. They show sensitivity to other peoples' emotions and needs.

Both nationally and internationally there have been numerous programs introduced into schools to promote greater student empathy. Los Angeles has spent over a million dollars introducing Second Step: Student Success Through Prevention. Other districts have brought in KIPP (Knowledge is Power Program) and David Levine's Teaching Empathy. While some skeptics of these programs question whether empathy can actually be taught, the anecdotal results suggest that these programs may have a significant influence on school culture, but in a rather unplanned and unusual way.

Public School 114 in the Bronx introduced a program to teach middle school students empathy in 2006. Since that time, the principal reports a 75 percent reduction in fights and disciplinary referrals. Before the workshops, she said teachers would immediately admonish the children for bad behavior and send them to the office; but since the empathy training began, they are more often sitting down with students and finding out what's wrong (Hu, 2009).

A 75 percent reduction in disciplinary referrals is a dramatic statistic and would suggest that empathy can indeed be learned (if not taught). However, if we read the principal's comments carefully, we recognize that she is attributing the reduction in disciplinary referrals not to students learning empathy, but to the teachers learning it. This is indeed the way to improve school culture—by enhancing teacher emotional intelligence.

In the classroom, focusing exclusively on others or self can be equally blinding and can produce misunderstanding and misinterpretation. What is required is an oscillating perspective that is both egocentric and allocentric: an "attentional" ballet in which we alternate and integrate paying close attention to self and others.

Teaching can be liberating. It can actually become a release from the cell of self-centeredness. Sonia Nieto (2005) writes, "Teaching helps make people more human. Much in the same way that becoming a parent may help make one less self-centered, more responsive to others, more aware of one's obligations beyond oneself, teaching too has this kind of effect" (p. 167).

Great teaching is not only liberating, it is inspiring.

INSPIRING OUR INSTINCT FOR ALTRUISM

There are some members of the scientific community who would deny the existence of altruism. They would look toward the "selfish gene" as a model of human behavior with, in our minds, unfortunate cynical consequences. If we accept the possibility of altruism, we may find its genesis in the "reciprocity" we witness in our closest relatives, the great apes.

Frans B. M. de Waal (as cited in Dalai Lama & Ekman, 2008) writes that reciprocity can be observed in experiments with captive chimpanzees in which food was given to individual chimps and then divided among others. Before giving the food, de Waal and others measured the spontaneous grooming of the chimp colony: Who grooms whom for how long?

Grooming is a pleasurable, relaxing activity and being groomed is much appreciated. In our experiment, we found that if one chimpanzee had groomed another, this greatly improved his chances of getting a share from the other. In other words, chimpanzees remember who has groomed them, returning the favor later on. Like humans, they seem to keep track of incoming and outgoing services. (p. 152)

Is it possible that as early humans began to separate stimulus and response, began to control impulsivity and delay gratification, that altruism developed as a more sophisticated form of reciprocity?

In his book *Before the Dawn,* Nicholas Wade (2006) paints a disturbing portrait of our prehistoric ancestors. In stark contrast to Jean-Jacques Rousseau's "noble savage," Wade suggests that our earliest predecessors were almost pathologically aggressive and violent—remorseless and determined killers of other protohuman species (e.g., the Neanderthals) and each other. Wade brings together archeological, anthropological, and genetic research and concludes that our earliest ancestors lived short, homicidal lives and were perpetually engaged in warfare against other tribes or clans. Contrary to what many of us would have guessed from a review of the history of the twentieth century (the hundred years that in 1970 Solzhenitsyn called the "cruelest century"), Wade asserts that throughout our evolution, humankind has become a more pacific, a more cooperative, and a social species.

Wade (2006) sees sociality emerging as an evolutionary stage of our human development in which we were able to recognize the survival benefits of reciprocity—in other words to calculate the cost-benefit ratio of cooperation as opposed to continued bloody warfare. He writes, "It is remarkable that this behavior [social cooperation] evolved at a time when primitive warfare was at its most intense and people had every reason to regard strangers with deep suspicion" (p. 162).

The genesis of social cooperation is trust, the glue that binds people together into clans or tribes. It is hard to overestimate the importance of social cooperation in evolutionary terms. Wade points out that without an innate willingness to trust strangers, human societies would still consist of family units of no more than a few dozen individuals. Towns and cities, in fact, any larger collective human endeavor, would be impossible.

Over our history, we have witnessed time and time again how collaborative work produces results that would be impossible for individuals to achieve on their own. The "pay off" for collective endeavor is exponentially greater than solo performance.

So is it possible that over time we humans have come to understand, perhaps at an instinctual level, that when we subjugate selfishness to a greater good, the benefits outweigh the sacrifice?

There is some evidence to suggest such an instinct.

Altruism resonates deeply with most of us. We have only to think of contagiousness of inspiration in the speeches of John F. Kennedy, Martin Luther King Jr., or Barack Obama to recognize how deeply we respond to the call of altruism. All of the world's major religions celebrate acts of selfless kindness and charity. The very word *inspiration* comes from the Latin word *inspirare* meaning to draw air into the lungs. Thus to inspire is to fill another person with noble or reverent emotions.

We would argue that it is the work of our teaching profession to inspire young people, and while there are numerous ways for us to accomplish this, connecting with our instinct for altruism is one of the most basic—our need to be needed.

THE SCHOOLGIRL AND THE SKINHEAD: INSPIRATION ON THE SUBWAY

An administrative colleague tells the story of leaving the school at the end of the day and making his way to the subway to go home. Once inside the train, he became aware of a "scene" that was transpiring at the other end of the carriage. A large, angry young man with a shaved head and swastika tattoo on his arm was loudly berating a small Somali woman. He was using highly offensive racist language and threatening physical gestures. The terrified Somali woman stared at her feet. The neo-Nazi barrage went on for several minutes until an eleven-year-old schoolgirl stood up and positioned herself directly between the skinhead and the Somali woman.

Our administrative colleague immediately recognized the girl as a student from his own school. He felt great anxiety for her safety and started to move toward the scene of the altercation.

The schoolgirl looked directly into the skinhead's eyes and calmly told him that his behavior was inappropriate. He was being hurtful, and he should stop. To everyone's surprise, the neo-Nazi did exactly that. He remained quiet until the next stop and then left the subway train.

Our administrative colleague spoke to the young girl after the incident. He asked her how she had come to make the decision to intervene in what might have been a dangerous situation. She replied that it had "just seemed the right thing to do." She said she hadn't thought about it very much, but then she made reference to the value of tolerance that her teacher had stressed in the classroom. Clearly, the inspiration of her teacher had been contagious to the young girl. In addition, the young girl's courage and conviction *inspired* our administrative colleague to tell and retell the story and inspired us to include it in this chapter.

Altruism is inspiring and highly contagious.

Activities, Exercises, and Case Studies That Develop Social Awareness and Empathy

"THE HOT SEAT": SENSITIZING OURSELVES TO NONVERBALS

Groups of four participants sit facing each other. There should be no table in between so that the nonverbal behavior can be easily viewed. Each participant will need a pen and piece of paper and a copy of the questions that he or she will ask (or the questions can be projected onto a screen. If they are, the person in the "hot seat" should sit with his or her back to the screen). Each member of the group is designated as A, B, C, or D.

There are four rounds in this activity. In each round, one person will be asked a question by each of the other three. While the person in the hot seat is responding, the other three participants will observe an assigned nonverbal behavior and record their observations. Participants rotate chairs at the end of each round.

Participant A will observe breathing.
Participant B will observe gestures and hands.
Participant C will observe the facial area—eye shifts, skin color, lip size.
Participant D will observe the torso and feet.

Round One Questions

- What has provided you with the greatest professional joy?
- What values keep you in education?
- Who do you feel contempt for?

Round Two Questions

- What was the biggest mistake you made as a child?
- Should gay marriages be legal?
- What professional obligations do you currently perform that are contrary to your beliefs?

Round Three Questions

- In what do you take greatest professional pride?
- All egos need gratification, what motivates yours?
- Under what conditions can we expect you to be deceitful?

Round Four Questions

- Which student has provided you with the greatest challenge?
- What causes you the greatest irritation with colleagues?
- What have you learned from a misjudgment in the classroom?

Following each round, the quartet debriefs on the nonverbal responses they have noticed. What patterns may be emerging?

Source: "The Hot Seat" is adapted from *Cognitive Coaching Foundation Seminar Learning Guide*, 7th ed., by Arthur Costa and Robert Garmston. Revised by Jane Ellison and Carolee Hays, 2007, pp. 94–97, Highlands Ranch, CO: Center for Cognitive Coaching.

ROUND-ROBIN REFLECTION

This activity is designed to encourage teams and work groups to reflect on how the members are working together. The activity focuses on social awareness and empathy and requires the participants to pay close attention to self and others in collaborative work settings.

At a certain point in a meeting or collaborative work session, the facilitator asks each team member to address two questions.

- What were some decisions that you made about when and how to participate in our work together today?
- What were some of the effects of those decisions on yourself and others?

In round-robin fashion, each member shares one decision and the effects of the decision. There is no cross talk. After each member shares a decision and the effect, the person to the right paraphrases the contribution. At the conclusion, the facilitator can debrief with the group by asking, "How did your decisions compare with what you intended?" or "What patterns are emerging?" or "What are some ways that you might apply this learning to future meetings?"

Source: From *The Adaptive School: A Sourcebook for Developing Collaborative Groups*, 2nd ed., by Robert Garmston and Bruce Wellman, 2009, Norwood, MA: Christopher-Gordon.

CASE STUDY

Directions: Please read the case study below and address the discussion questions that follow.

"LD or L2? That Is the Question"

Uta had joined the Abraham Lincoln Middle School at the start of the year. It was now November, and her teachers were concerned.

"I just don't think we have enough information," Lee Rawlings announced to the other members of the child-study team. There was a very audible edge of impatience to her voice. "I feel we are talking in circles. I'm sorry, but I do. We all want to do what is best for Uta. So why can't we just get on with it and test her?"

"What kind of testing are you suggesting?" Brenda Fellows, the school psychologist, asked gently.

"The usual kind. You know, the WISC whatever-it-is." Lee's frustration was visible in her expression. "The one that gives you a cognitive IQ. I mean, how do we begin to know Uta's potential without knowing how bright she is? We need the results of a cognitive test."

"But with the language issue and the cultural bias of the test itself . . . ," Sam Littlewood interjected.

Rene Mylar noted the irritation in Lee's voice and decided it was time for her, as chair, to intervene. "Let me try to summarize where we are. Uta is a fifth-grade student who entered this school about four months ago. Originally Uta is from Latvia, but her mother tongue is Russian, which she speaks at home with Mom and Dad . . ."

"But she's not ESL," Bernadette Shetty announced. "Virtually all her previous schooling has been in English."

"That's correct," Rene conceded with a smile. "Prior to her arrival in the United States, Uta was enrolled in the Interfaith Christian Academy in Kanu, northern Nigeria. Her father was a missionary. The instruction was in English, but we don't know the quality of English."

"Uta may not be ESL as defined by our policy, but she may still be struggling with English."

"There could also be a learning disability," Bernadette suggested.

Sam nodded, "LD or L2? Now there's a knotty question!"

"I agree with Lee," Brenda Fellows commented, which actually surprised the rest of the child-study team members because only moments before she had been arguing against testing Uta. "I agree with Lee that we don't have enough information about Uta. I think that's the topic we should be focusing on—the collection of useful information."

Rene smiled at her colleagues around the table. She seized the moment, "Can we all agree with Brenda's suggestion that the collection of useful data should be our primary focus?" Heads around the table nodded in assent. "Does anyone have a suggestion for how this might take place?"

"We know she's having trouble in reading and writing. Would it be helpful to give her an achievement test in reading?" Sam asked. "We could also look at a sample of her writing and try to identify areas of weakness."

"Good suggestions," Rene murmured.

"I would also be in favor of some clinical observations," Brenda added.

"Clinical observations? That sounds scary." Lee suppressed a chuckle.

"I would go into a classroom and observe Uta with some specific questions in mind," Brenda suggested.

"What kind of questions?" Lee asked.

"For example, how does Uta function in English with her peers? In what settings does she function best? In large groups, small groups, or with individual work? I would try to develop a learning profile for Uta," Brenda added.

"We could also probably get some useful information from the parents," Bernadette suggested. "We could ask them about Uta's functioning in Russian."

Rene held up her hands to call for silence: "I think we should pause here for a moment. We have three excellent suggestions on the table: achievement testing in reading and the diagnostic assessment of a writing sample, clinical observations in the classroom setting, and a carefully structured parent interview. Sam, could you conduct the reading test?" Sam nodded. "Perhaps Bernadette and Lee could look at a sample of Uta's writing. Brenda, I assume you would be prepared to undertake some clinical observations?" Brenda nodded. "I will invite the parents in for a conference. Is there anyone who would like to help me plan the interview with Mom and Dad?"

Lee raised her hand.

"Great. Thank you, Lee. So we have an initial data-collection plan. I suggest we place Uta on our agenda for two weeks time. At that time we can share our reports and analyze the data. Thank you all."

Discussion Questions

1. What evidence do you see in the case study of empathy?

2. How do the characters exhibit social awareness?

3. What emotionally intelligent behavior do you see in the case study?

7 Orchestrating Our Relationships

Creating a Supportive Learning Environment

The best teachers make student voices the center of the class.

—Landsman, Moore, and Simmons (2008, p. 63)

Building meaningful relationships means becoming vulnerable to the silliness of nine-year-olds, being open to them, and allowing them insight to your humor and humility. It means sharing yourself in a way that makes the teacher a real person, with deep feelings about life and humanity. . . . The more real I am to my students, the more open they are to me. When I nurture this kind of relationship it carries over into the kind of learning that blossoms into life-changing moments and revolutionary thinking.

—Elaine Stinson (as cited in Nieto, 2005, p. 109)

The challenges of relationship management within the classroom are complex and different from other social situations. As Stinson suggests in the above quotation, nurturing meaningful learning relationships in the classroom is about being open and emotionally authentic. At the same time, teachers can never forget that they are teachers, and therefore, such openness and authenticity needs to be tempered with a degree of calculation and premeditation.

So where to begin?

Empathy is certainly a starting point but is insufficient in and of itself. Teachers orchestrate relationships in the classroom to foster the trust that facilitates learning. In this chapter, we will examine how teachers navigate various emotional geographies and overcome obstacles to trust. We will explore three different types of trust and look at how the contagiousness of emotions can affect these. Finally, we will address one of the most vexing questions that emotionally intelligent teachers wrestle with: "What does a teacher do with an unlikable child?"

EMPATHY IS ONLY A STARTING POINT: BOUNDARY MANAGEMENT

Many years ago, Bill had a young teaching colleague named Craig. Like Bill, Craig was a high school English teacher. During the time they worked together, Craig was a paragon of social awareness. Perhaps as a result of a difficult divorce that he was embroiled in, Craig was hypersensitive to his own emotional needs and those of his students. Every day during lunch, Craig would listen to a group of high school girls describe the problems of their personal lives. Craig would listen intently and then offer anecdotes from his own private life that mirrored those of his students. Craig was supremely empathetic and a deeply reflective listener, but he lacked boundary management. While there was no question that he cared deeply about those he interacted with, he allowed himself to become confused about his role—that of a teacher or that of a sympathetic friend.

Ultimately, Craig's role confusion actually undermined his positive influence with his students. As the details of Craig's tempestuous divorce became known to his students, the students themselves became increasingly uncomfortable with the degree of intimacy. One day during lunch, Craig shared with a group of students that over the past two years he and his wife had been trying to conceive a child. Their failure to do so had caused recriminations and had led to their separation. At the end of Craig's description, one of the students asked, "Do we need to know all this?" The following morning the girl's mother was in the principal's office complaining that Craig had, in her words, "crossed the line."

And of course, Craig had crossed the line that separates professional relationships from intimate friendships. Whatever empathetic strengths Craig may have had, his personal emotional needs made him blind to how relationships need to operate within a school. His self-disclosure had moved from the appropriate realm which promotes trust, into the realm where it caused the recipients discomfort and anxiety.

Empathy by itself is not sufficient to foster a supportive learning environment. We must also understand the expectations of our roles and navigate through various emotional geographies.

NAVIGATING EMOTIONAL GEOGRAPHIES

Andy Hargreaves (2001) identifies five domains that can challenge teacher-student relationships. He refers to these as emotional geographies. Each geography represents potential distancing factors that teachers need to overcome to establish emotional bonds with their students. Hargreaves is clear that "successful teaching and learning . . . depends on establishing close bonds with students and creating conditions of teaching that make emotional understanding possible" (p. 1060).

Hargreaves' emotional geographies include (1) sociocultural distance, (2) moral distance, (3) professional distance, (4) political distance, and (5) physical distance.

1. Sociocultural Distance

Schools are filled with students from many different cultural backgrounds, and in many cases, the culture of the teacher will be different from those of the students. There may also be socioeconomic class differences. The sociocultural distance between teacher and students can lead to stereotypes of students and the misinterpretation of motives.

Popkewitz (1998) suggests that such stereotypes may result from our assumptions regarding the superiority or normality of our culture in comparison with others. While it has become politically incorrect to overtly hold that our culture is in some way superior to someone else's, many teachers hold subconsciously to the notion that our own culture is "normal" and other cultures are in some fashion curiosities or even aberrations. Becoming a culturally competent teacher means experiencing a culture that is not your own and suspending judgment. It means seeking out the commonalities between cultures rather than simply focusing on the differences.

2. Moral Distance

Moral distance is created when there are conflicting purposes between teachers, students and their parents, and administrators. When teachers believe that their purposes in the classroom are not understood, are not valued, or worse yet, are being threatened, negative emotions can be generated and relationships can be seriously damaged. When teachers perceive that their purposes are at odds with those around them, anxiety, frustration, and anger result.

Hargreaves' study found that the strongest source of negative teacher emotion resulted from parents questioning or criticizing their academic purposes, judgment, expertise, and basic professionalism.

On the other hand, when there is "moral agreement" about the purposes of education between teachers, parents, administrators, board members, and students, there is a mutual sense of support and appreciation that releases energy, fosters creativity, and dramatically lowers stress on all concerned—including students.

3. Professional Distance

The principle of professional distance is intended to protect both parties from the volatile and less-than-predictable influence of emotions when we are carrying out our professional responsibilities. Maintaining distance means perceiving the other person in terms of his or her role (e.g., patient, client, student).

Hargreaves perceives an inherent contradiction in the concept of *professionalism* as we think of it in terms of teaching. He recognizes that school teaching requires a "feminine caring ethic." Many, if not most, of the responsibilities of teachers demand a high degree of emotional understanding. This is not only the case with teacher-student relationships, but also with relationships between teachers and parents, and teachers and administrators. However, the conventional concept of professionalism, drawn from the traditional male domains of medicine and law, requires that professionals avoid emotional connections with patients and clients. In fact, one of the hallmarks of professionals is the emotional distance they maintain from clients. So teachers are placed in the odd position of being expected to care for their students in a somewhat clinical and detached manner. Goleman (2006) writes that "people in helping professions must work hard to ensure that the ingredients of rapport operate during their professional encounters. Their detachment needs to be balanced with sufficient empathy" (p. 112).

4. Political Distance

Hargreaves uses the term *political* to refer to the dynamics of power within the school and more specifically in the classroom. Where does the authority lie? On what is the power based? And how is it used and to what end?

When Bill was growing up in Britain in the 1950s, the power dynamic in the classroom was fairly straightforward. Teachers were, for the most part, unabashedly authoritarian. They established control over the students in their classes by issuing orders and edicts; they motivated children by the use of fear, and they punished bad behavior or what they perceived to be a lack of effort by public ridicule and the infliction of physical pain. Compliance was the order of the day.

Fortunately, today the situation is different.

We recognize the connection between our feelings of power or powerlessness and our emotions. We have only to recall the presence of an authoritarian teacher in our childhood classroom or the times we worked for a dictatorial principal for the feelings of anger, frustration, shame, anxiety, and depression to return. If we hold an external authority responsible for our diminished potency, we tend to feel anger and we may rebel. On the other hand, if we hold ourselves responsible for our powerlessness, we tend to feel shame and possibly self-pity. If we cannot see a way to enhance our efficacy, we tend to drift into depression.

On the other hand, when our efficacy increases, we tend to feel enhanced status which results in happiness, satisfaction, and contentment.

It takes a degree of courage for a teacher to relinquish control of what gets done, said, or thought in the classroom. We would suggest that there is an important distinction between the management of student behavior and the control of student thought. We probably have all encountered the "guess-what-I'm-thinking" teacher. This is the teacher who knows the answer or outcome that he wants and asks students questions until they have succeeded in guessing what he is thinking. Judith Baker (as cited in Nieto, 2005) sees this intellectual manipulation as an insidious form of thought control. She questions the negative effect that teachers may have on student thought with their seemingly endless leading questions. "If this goes on for many years, the K–12 interruption of thought must be truly debilitating" (p. 211). Baker's solution is to stop asking questions (homework questions, test questions, raise-your-hand-and-answer-this questions). Instead she asks her students to *notice*. What are you noticing? Her subtle but important shift in questioning provides multiple access points and does not control student thinking.

The dynamics of power and authority play out daily in classrooms around the world. When teachers manage their classrooms in such a manner that they diminish the power of their students, they create political distance and, consequently, impede trust and learning. Effective classroom management does not need to be based on the teacher's position of power. On the contrary, the most effective classroom management is based on clear expectations, often negotiated between teacher and students, of purpose, individual rights, collective welfare, and respectful behavior.

5. Physical Distance

While absence may make the heart grow fonder, proximity certainly enhances emotional understanding. In other words, the more contact we have with other persons the more likely we are to come to understand them. This is true of teachers' relationships with students, parents, and administrators. However, as students grow older, our physical proximity with them diminishes. Rather than spending all day together, as teacher and students often do in the elementary school, secondary schoolteachers may see students for only fifty minutes a day or perhaps only three or four times a week. With the decreased proximity, emotional understanding becomes more challenging.

The purpose of navigating these emotional geographies is to develop a learning environment based upon trust.

THE ROLE OF TRUST

Arguably, the most influential variable in any collective human endeavor is the presence or absence of interpersonal trust. Schools and classrooms are no exception. When we talk about relationship management and creating a supportive learning environment, we are really talking about the development and maintenance of communal trust. There are few more important endeavors that teachers or school leaders can engage in.

In the course of a year, we visit and work in between twenty and thirty different schools. Most of these schools have cultures that are based on trust. And for the most part, the members of the schools' community take that trust for granted. This is because trust only becomes an issue in schools when it is damaged or absent.

On occasion, we will visit a school where trust is absent. It is not a pleasant experience. Suspicion and anxiety fill the void. Teachers and administrators do not presume positive intentions of each other. There is an absence of good faith. Gossip and rumors are rife, and a toxic culture pervades the schoolhouse.

There are some astonishing qualities to such toxic cultures. They can be seductive and, despite the fact that virtually everyone recognizes that they are corrosive, they are highly resistant to change. Michael Thompson (2000) suggests that over time schools create for themselves "narratives" and the inhabitants of the schoolhouse then "live" that story. We literally define our professional reality by the stories that we tell ourselves. These narratives can be positive or negative. When a school has habitually told itself a negative narrative, a toxic culture can come to exist. The toxicity can manifest itself in antagonistic relationships between teachers and administration, teachers and students, and parents and school personnel. Coupled with poor relationships, we also see the emergence of pessimism and cynicism.

What is also astonishing in such schools is that many of the teachers and administrators, while acknowledging the existence of the toxic culture, will claim that it is not having a negative effect on student learning. In our experience, this is never the case. When trust is damaged, it invariably impacts negatively on student learning.

Harvard Professor Emeritus Roland Barth (1990) brings the issue of trust into fine focus. He suggests that a remarkably accurate barometer of student learning in the classroom is the quality of adult-to-adult relationships in the schoolhouse. Barth argues that if we observe the way in which adults share craft knowledge (or don't), plan together (or separately), solve problems and manage conflicts (or exacerbate them), we can forge a pretty precise idea of the quality of learning that is taking place in the classroom. Obviously, the foundation of high-quality adult-to-adult relationships is emotional intelligence and trust.

THE THREE FLAVORS OF TRUST

Researchers Bryk and Schneider (2004), working in the Chicago school system, identified three types of trust, which they labeled *organic, contractual,* and *relational.* Organic trust is the type of trust that people have in their religious beliefs. Organic trust is based on implicit faith. Bryk and Schneider concluded that this was not the type of trust that could permeate the culture of most schools.

Contractual trust is the type of trust that you want to have with the builder who is constructing your new house. You want the quantity surveyor to spell out exactly how many electrical outlets you will have in the kitchen and that the fixtures in the bathroom will be porcelain and not plastic. When the builder hands you the front door keys, you do not want any unpleasant surprises. Not surprisingly, Bryk and Schneider (2004) also concluded that contractual trust was inappropriate and unrealistic as a cohesive force in school culture. In fact, a reliance on contractual trust in schools can act to undermine relationships and morale.

Bryk and Schneider (2004) suggest that healthy schools have strong cultures of relational trust. Teachers, administrators, students, and parents understand their respective roles and responsibilities and how these interact. They also have confidence that others will live up to both explicit and implicit expectations of those relationships.

Should teachers set out to deliberately develop relational trust with their students? We believe so. However, some teachers worry that by doing so they will "waste" valuable instructional time. Class time should never be wasted. However, trusting relationships can actually make accessing the curriculum more efficient in that students feel emotionally invested in the classroom.

THE CHEMISTRY OF TRUST

Biologically, trust is to some extent contingent on two hormones: oxytocin and vasopressin. Both are emerging as having a powerful influence on our social behaviors. Oxytocin, the so-called bonding chemical, has been shown to promote affiliative behavior. It generates a feeling of relaxed satisfaction and actually mimics the addictive pleasures of opiate drugs in the brain. Interestingly, on average women have more oxytocin than men. Researchers (Wade, 2006) have found that oxytocin substantially increases the level of trust. In other words, oxytocin significantly increases an individual's willingness to accept social risks that might be encountered in interpersonal relationships.

While trust may make us feel good, it is not about some warm fuzziness. Trust is about recognizing how we invariably depend upon other people and how we can enhance relationships by decreasing our personal sense of vulnerability.

OBSTACLES TO TRUST:
A VERB DISGUISED AS A NOUN

There are several structural obstacles to the development of trust in classrooms and schools. The first is that trust is a nominalization—that is a process that is spoken about as though it were a static and unchanging thing or event—a verb disguised as a noun. Verbs, especially gerunds (the *ing* form, *trusting*), imply engagement and participation by individuals. Garmston and Wellman (2009) write, "Some groups tell us that trust is missing in their organization. Groups cannot improve trust: They can only increase trusting behaviors. We've learned to ask what people will be doing and saying when they are 'trusting'" (p. 143). What we can envision, we can also develop.

The second obstacle to developing classroom trust is the teacher's role as an evaluator. While assessment comes with the territory of teaching, it can inhibit the growth of trust on the part of students. Many teachers feel a similar ambivalence toward their supervisors when the time comes for their annual professional evaluation. Dickerson and Kemeny (as cited in Goleman, 2006) suggest that when we are evaluated by another person our social self is threatened. The social self is the way we come to view ourselves through other people's eyes. We receive hundreds, perhaps thousands, of messages each day from other people focused on how they perceive us. These messages help to form our self-image and our sense of self-worth. When that social self is judged negatively, our sense of self-worth is threatened. We may feel that we are less than desirable. We may even feel shamed or rejected.

There are several ways that teachers can reduce the negative impact on relationships caused by their role as evaluators. First, we can emphasize to our students that we are assessing their work and their achievement *not* their being. To do this we must avoid placing our own negative interpretations on a child's motivation (e.g., "He's just not trying," "She's bone idle").

Second, we can employ descriptive feedback as opposed to evaluative feedback. Descriptive feedback might include "Your essay had a captivating introduction, but lacked a meaningful conclusion" or "You maintained eye contact with your audience throughout your oral presentation." Evaluative feedback might include grades, such as A+ or C−, or comments like "good job" or "well done." The most important difference between descriptive and evaluative feedback is that descriptive feedback is essential for efficient student learning (it represents the data upon which students and teachers can scaffold new learning). Evaluative feedback is entirely extraneous to learning. In fact, in most cases, it signals to a student that the piece of work or project is finished, can be filed and never thought about again. Descriptive feedback, on the other hand, sends the message that the teacher wants the student to improve. Accordingly, it builds trust.

Third, we can find something positive to comment upon. Every child does something well. If we have trouble finding that "something," the fault probably lies within the construction of our perceptions.

Fourth, and perhaps most important, we can provide support and guidance in student self-assessment. Truly, the only value in any assessment is the degree to which it promotes healthy and accurate self-assessment. This is the life skill that we want students to take away from our classrooms. As counterintuitive as it may seem, there is no evidence to suggest that external, evaluative feedback promotes personal growth. In fact, Carol Sanford's research (1995, as cited in Garmston, 2005) actually suggests that external feedback is negatively correlated with accuracy in self-evaluation and with learning to manage oneself.

Studies of both schoolchildren and employees at DuPont and Colgate-Palmolive (Sanford, 1995, as cited in Garmston, 2005) reveal some startling findings about the use of external feedback. In the first case, two groups of nine- and ten-year-old children were studied in terms of the accuracy with which they were able to describe their own behavior. Before the research began, most of the children were not able to report accurately on personal behavior. "They would vehemently defend the rightness of their self-observations even when faced with indisputable evidence such as film and recordings" (p. 205).

The first group of children worked with adult instructors who used video and audio recordings to improve the students' accuracy of observation. The instructors employed praise and correction as part of their feedback.

The second group worked with instructors who never gave any feedback:

> They continually asked each student to self-reflect on how well his or her behavior matched the stated procedure. Group 2 instructors did not correct student perceptions or provide outside evidence. In the beginning, the students' accuracy was very low. After a few weeks, the students' reflections became increasingly accurate and *more accurate* [emphasis added] than students in Group 1. (Sanford, 1995, as cited in Garmston, 2005, p. 206)

Very similar findings result from feedback sessions with adults. In an effort to improve productivity, members of work teams at DuPont and Colgate-Palmolive listened to feedback from colleagues, supervisors, and subordinates (360° feedback) on how they might improve their work performance. The objective of the sessions was to enhance the understanding of how one individual might impact others and generally to improve teamwork. According to Garmston (2005), "The exact opposite occurred. Feedback processes were found to undermine these goals and produce nonproductive side effects. DuPont and Colgate-Palmolive are now committed to practices that help to build their capability for self-reflection and self-assessment" (p. 206).

Sanford (1995, as cited in Garmston, 2005), Kohn (1999), and Joyce and Showers (1980) each make the observation that external feedback actually reduces the capacity for accurate self-reflection.

TRUST AND EMOTIONAL CONTAGION

Emotions are as contagious as viruses—both positive and negative emotions. But the negative emotions can be particularly destructive in schools. On a collegial level, we have all witnessed such contagion in the faculty lounge when our chronically negative colleague moans about the "hopeless kids" or the "dysfunctional parents." We've also seen how habitual naysayers can suck the energy and vitality out of a staff meeting—"We tried that ten years ago. It didn't work then, and it won't work now." In short, we know that teachers' moods, emotions, and overall dispositions can have a powerful impact on job performance, decision making, creativity, turnover, teamwork, and leadership (Barsade & Gibson, 2007). Our emotions are contagious and influence the degree to which trust is present in schools.

In 1985, researchers Howes, Hokanson, and Lowenstein conducted a study on the infectiousness of depression at Florida State University. Incoming students to the university were given the Beck Depression Inventory. Those who registered little or no depression were assigned a mildly depressed roommate. These students were retested periodically over the next three months. Those students who had been assigned a mildly depressed roommate became themselves more depressed over time. Elaine Hatfield (Hatfield, Cacioppo, & Rapson, 1994) writes that "these findings are a bit unsettling. They suggest that depressed physicians, nurses, and teachers, for example, might have a depressing effect on their charges, at a time when they are especially vulnerable" (p. 102). The implications for the classroom teacher are significant. Emotions are contagious, and there is a direct correlation between the degree of "infectiousness" and the power and influence of the individual. Low-status individuals who enjoy little authority or influence are not nearly as emotionally contagious as individuals who occupy positions of leadership. Powerful leaders have enormous emotional influence. We have only to look at charismatic political, religious, or community leaders to see the veracity of this. Emotions flow from the dominant to the less influential.

Teachers are by definition the leaders of the classroom, and we wield very significant power and influence. Therefore, teachers can be highly emotionally infectious. Depending upon the emotions that the teacher brings to the classroom, this can be a positive and constructive experience that fosters a supportive learning community, or in the case of a teacher suffering from chronic stress, depression, anger-management issues, or personal problems, a very significant impediment to student learning.

Emotional contagion is the primary mechanism through which emotions are shared. More often than not, emotional contagion occurs without conscious knowledge, although it can also be consciously induced, for example, in theater, movies, dance, or music performances (Barsade & Gibson, 2007).

Emotional contagion is present whenever two or more people are relating well. Psychologists call this primitive emotional contagion *synchrony* and suggest that it is relatively "automatic, unintentional, uncontrollable and largely inaccessible to conversant awareness" (Hatfield et al., 1994, p. 5). An example of synchrony is the manner in which people who are relating well mimic each other's nonverbal behavior. This is seen in posture, eye contact, gesture, tone of voice, accent, breathing patterns, and even in the metaphors that we may subconsciously use to match the representational system of the other person.

While researchers have found that power and emotional contagion are negatively correlated (i.e., the powerful do not seem to be infected by the emotions of the powerless), people in the "caring" professions (e.g., medicine, social work, teaching) who have a psychological investment in the welfare of their clients are particularly vulnerable to both synchrony and emotional contagion. Thus, while teachers can and do "infect" their students with their moods, the reverse also appears to occur: Teachers can "catch" their students' emotions.

On average, women are more emotionally expressive than men. In a meta-analysis of gender differences in emotional expressiveness, Judith Hall (1984, as cited in Hatfield et al., 1994) found that women are more open and expressive than are men. They are better encoders of emotions such as happiness, love, fear, surprise, and dominance. Women are also more effective senders of emotional messages. They are more spontaneous with laughter, smiles, touch, eye contact, and facial expression.

Haviland and Malatesta (1981) trace the difference in emotional expressiveness to infancy. They found that from birth boys appeared to be far less effective than girls at interpreting other's emotions. To interpret nonverbal clues of emotional states, one must first pay attention to them (otherwise, we would simply miss the cues). Haviland and Malatesta found that infant females were much more attentive to the emotional expressions of others. Girls would make eye contact faster and maintain it for longer periods of time. "Women were simply better at reading what is meant by the awkward glance, superior smile, or hesitant speech. Their advantage was most pronounced for facial cues, less pronounced for bodily cues, and least pronounced for vocal cues." (Hatfield et al., 1994, p. 162).

MIRROR NEURONS AND EMOTIONAL CONTAGION

Emotional contagion both in the classroom and in the outside world may have its roots in a recent scientific discovery: mirror neurons.

We have known for many years that imitation has played a crucial role in human evolution—in our learning and in our socialization. What we haven't known until very recently is how imitative learning works. We can now speculate on the mechanism by which emotions are contagious. Both processes seem to rely on mirror neurons.

Mirror neurons were discovered by accident at the University of Parma in Italy in the mid-1990s. Professor Giacomo Rizzolatti (Iacoboni, 2008) and his research team had attached electrodes to the brains of monkeys and were mapping the neural activity as the monkeys reacted to different stimuli.

The eureka moment was totally unexpected. One member of Rizzolatti's (Iacoboni, 2008) research team returned to the laboratory after the working day was over. The monkeys were still connected to the electrodes. The research assistant picked up a peanut from the table, and to his astonishment, the monkeys' brains fired as though they—not he—had picked up the peanut. The researcher could hardly believe what he had witnessed. The neuron didn't seem to know the difference between performing the act and watching it being performed. And so the new neuron was dubbed the mirror neuron.

Since that time, researchers in California (Iacoboni, 2008; Ramachandran, 2000) and elsewhere in the world have greatly expanded on this remarkable discovery. Scientists have found that the density of mirror neurons in human brains is considerably greater than in monkeys and their location is much more widespread—most noticeably in the areas of the brain associated with empathy and perception. In 1998, dense clusters of mirror neurons were found in the Broca's area of the brain—the region which is critical for language production. Mirror neurons help us understand the contagiousness of yawns, laughter, and good and bad moods. Mirror neurons may also help explain our edge-of-the-seat excitement while watching a tense sports match or a suspenseful movie. Because mirror neurons cannot tell the difference between observing and performing, we experience the Superbowl as though we were making the touchdown!

Iacoboni (2008) from UCLA conjectures that mirror neurons provide the foundation upon which we build empathy, compassion, morality, and ultimately trust.

There can be no question that imitative learning is one of the most powerful and effective means by which we acquire new skills and knowledge. Accordingly, we suggest that the traditional isolation of teachers from one another in schools may be the greatest hubris of our profession (Powell & Kusuma-Powell, 2007a). Traditionally, schools were structured on the model of an egg crate. Egg crates are great for eggs. They keep eggs separate from each other in transit and therefore prevent cracking and damage. Egg crates are a much less satisfactory model for schools. Teacher isolation from each other stands in the way of imitative learning and emotional intelligence.

WHAT'S A TEACHER TO DO?

How does a teacher develop a trusting, emotionally intelligent classroom?

Researchers in trust in schools have identified four criteria for discernment (Bryk & Schneider, 2004). Criteria for discernment are what we use to determine whether or not a person is trustworthy. The four criteria for discernment are respect, competence, personal regard, and integrity. Each of these is embedded to some extent in every decision a teacher makes in the classroom.

Let's observe how these criteria for discernment may play out in a teacher's daily routine. Clearly the influence of each criteria will be determined to a large extent by the developmental age of the child. For example, integrity will be understood differently from the perspective of a first grader than from that of a high school student.

DISCERNMENT IN ACTION: GROUPING, MEDIATION, AND CARING

One of a teacher's primary areas of responsibility is the formation, implementation, and coordination of networks of children engaged in learning. The teacher is involved in a multitude of decisions that relate to the social management of the classroom: How large or small should the groups be? Given the specific learning objectives, what is the best composition of groups? Should there be a balance of different intelligences? Learning styles? Interests? Linguistic groups? Genders? Emerging leadership potentials? How will complementary personalities and temperaments come into play?

How teachers group students can send subtle messages about their trustworthiness. If teachers group students exclusively or even primarily by perceived ability, it will send a message of disrespect to those placed in the lower ability groups. This will inhibit the building of trust.

Teachers are often called upon to assume the role of mediator: a metaphorical boundary official attempting to keep conflict in the cognitive domain (about ideas and issues) as opposed to the affective domain (about personalities and emotions). She is engaged in helping children to differentiate between constructive conflict—the exchange of ideas that broadens perceptions and enhances learning—and destructive conflict, which undermines relationships and damages trust. She is constantly asking questions, such as "Has the debate reached a point where I need to put a stop to it?" "When is consensus appropriate?" "Is this a decision that I can share with my students?" or "Is compromise an option?" The teacher is making hundreds of such decisions daily. She is modeling the life skills that children will need as they emerge into adulthood. How teachers resolve classroom conflicts also sends messages about their trust-worthiness. Teachers who resolve conflicts capriciously, or in less than an evenhanded manner, may be perceived as playing favorites and thus lacking in integrity.

Learning is profoundly influenced by the teacher's personal regard. This is the teacher's ability to recognize and respond appropriately to students' feelings and concerns. Another word for personal regard may be "caring." While this is a critical feature of primary school classrooms, it is true for students of all ages. If students perceive that the teacher cares, trust will be developed.

Trust is not something that we accomplish and then hang on the wall like a plaque or trophy. It is a process and a journey, and along the way, we will almost certainly meet negative and positive emotional overrides.

POSITIVE AND NEGATIVE EMOTIONAL OVERRIDES

Gottman (as cited in Gladwell, 2005) suggests that in each interpersonal relationship there is a distinctive "signature" that emerges. Often the signature is so subtle that we are not consciously aware of it; but it is nevertheless present—sometimes obviously so to external observers. This is also true of learning relationships between teachers and students within the classroom.

One of the most distinctive features of such a signature is what Gottman (as cited in Gladwell, 2005) refers to as positive or negative emotional overrides. A positive emotional override buffers the relationship against irritability. When the teacher is impatient or short-tempered, the student will dismiss the incident by thinking, "Oh, he's just a bit grumpy today." The implication is that the teacher's irritability is a temporary aberration in what is otherwise a constructive and trusting relationship. This illustrates the power of a positive emotional override.

A negative emotional override, in contrast, will result in relatively neutral behavior being perceived as negative. In the negative override state, people draw lasting conclusions about each other. An example of a negative emotional override might be when the teacher compliments Mary on a piece of work and Julia interprets it as just another example of the teacher's habitual favoritism. "Mary's always the teacher's pet. She can't do anything wrong."

Gottman (as cited in Gladwell, 2005) has identified four characteristic behaviors of the negative emotional override state: defensiveness, stonewalling, criticism, and contempt. Of these, the most powerfully destructive is contempt. Expressions of contempt, through inappropriate humor and sarcasm, are the death knell to any learning relationship. "Contempt is closely related to disgust, and what disgust and contempt are about is completely rejecting and excluding someone from the community" (Goleman, 2006, p. 30).

To become aware of positive and negative emotional override states, teachers need to uncover the process through which they construct their perceptions of students and their individual learning potential.

So what is the unspeakable negative emotional override? Let's end the chapter with the question that dare not speak its name.

WHAT DOES A TEACHER DO WITH AN UNLIKABLE CHILD?

An unlikable child? For some, the phrase may read like heresy, and they may deny the existence of such a student. "In twenty years of teaching, I can honestly say I have never met a child I disliked." For others, the concept may be apparently irrelevant. "I'm in the classroom to teach, not to like or dislike children." But for many, perhaps even most teachers, the presence of an unlikable child is or has been a reality—and probably one of the child's parents' worst nightmares.

Neuroscience now suggests to us that nature and nurture have a bidirectional influence on each other. Not only do our genes influence our social behavior, but our behavior (and our social environment) actually influence our genes. Children who have a genetic disposition toward friendliness and warmth will respond in kind and so a positive cycle can be initiated. However, the opposite can also occur. A child's genetics can produce a temperament that is irritable and aggressive. In this case, the parents and teachers may also respond in kind. This may take the form of emotional aggression or harsh discipline. This pattern may actually exacerbate the child's inappropriate behavior and so evoke more and more teacher negativity. And so a vicious, destructive cycle may be initiated.

So let's return to the awkward question of what a teacher is to do with an unlikable child. First of all, we would suggest that the teacher do nothing *with the child*. While some children are obstinate, arrogant, stubborn, unruly, lacking respect, even violent, the antipathy the teacher may be feeling is not produced by the child but rather is an emotional reaction fashioned by the teacher.

The first step is to recognize the emotional effect that the child's behavior is having on us.

A "HANDFUL" CALLED JONATHAN

Jonathan has recently transferred into Karen's fourth-grade class. The previous teacher called him a "handful" and rolled her eyes when Karen asked about parent support. Jonathan is the nine-year-old son of the regional vice president of a major international bank. Jonathan wears designer children's clothing, and he is collected from school daily by a chauffeur-driven Mercedes. Jonathan never says "please" or "thank you" and has great difficulty delaying gratification. He is impatient, demanding, and quick to anger. When he doesn't get his own way, he either bullies his classmates or is prone to sulk. He doesn't pick up after himself, and his needs are most often expressed in the form of demands.

Jonathan has managed to get under Karen's skin.

Karen grew up in the South Bronx. Her mother was a single parent who worked as a food handler in the school cafeteria. Karen's mother was determined that her children would have more opportunities than she had. Karen watched her mother sacrifice so that she and her three siblings could finish high school and, in Karen's case, go to university.

After two weeks in class with Jonathan, Karen's impression of him is that he is an arrogant, spoiled little rich kid. But Karen doesn't stop there. She also notices something else. She notices that the other children in her class seem to share the same impression of Jonathan, and this makes them avoid him—especially at lunchtime and recess. She also notices that

Jonathan wants to play with the other children but doesn't seem to know how. She comes to understand that Jonathan is also a lonely little boy who would love to have friends but doesn't yet have the social skills to do so. This insight allows Karen to move the focus of her attention from her own irritation with Jonathan's superior attitude to how she is constructing her perception of him.

On this subject, Art Costa and Bob Garmston (2002) offer some sage advice from their work in *Cognitive Coaching.* They make two powerful suggestions. The first is that we might approach such a situation with deliberately crafted positive presuppositions. We might attempt to reframe our perceptions in more positive language. Thus the stubborn child might be conceived of as persistent or the unruly child as field independent. Jonathan's disrespectful behavior came to be understood by Karen as a result of wanting friends but as yet lacking the skills with which to develop them. *This is not simple word play.* The positive reframing of perceptions allows us emotional disengagement, the all-important suspension of judgment, and an opportunity to uncover strengths in the student that may not have been previously obvious.

Second, Costa and Garmston (2002) suggest to us that people make the best decisions available to them at the time. Does this mean that a student's decision not to study for a math test was a good one? Of course not, but given the child's history of struggling with math, the student may perceive that a failure caused by a lack of study may be less injurious to her self-esteem than a failure preceded by real effort on her part. When we accept that students make the best decisions available to them at the time, our perceptions move from simplistic labels into a rich landscape of potential understanding.

In coming to know ourselves as teachers, we need to critically examine our "default positions." The notion of default position is a metaphor taken from the technological age. On a computer, the default position is the program that automatically is engaged unless the machine is specifically instructed otherwise. In the classroom, our default positions are those routine instructional behaviors or responses that "kick in" when we are not consciously thinking about them or even aware of their existence. Whatever has become habitual or automatic in the classroom is worthy of critical examination.

Developing our emotional intelligence as teachers is challenging but gratifying work. In our next chapter, we will examine some ways that we can bring together the various aspects of this challenge.

Activities, Exercises, and Case Studies That Develop a Supportive Learning Community

LISTENING IS AN ACTIVE VERB: PARAPHRASING AND PROBING

Active listening sets a tone of respect in the classroom and contributes to trust. One way in which teachers can practice and model active listening is by paraphrasing student contributions to small-group or class discussions. When teachers paraphrase a student's contribution to a class discussion, they send three vitally important emotional messages.

1. I am listening to you

2. I understand or I am trying to understand you

3. I care about you and what you have to say

Paraphrasing dignifies and honors the student. This is particularly powerful when we work with children who believe they have low social status. Cohen and Lotan (1997) observe that classrooms have social hierarchies and that children who believe they have high status learn more effectively than children who believe they have low status. They also observe that teachers can mediate the status of children. We can do this by publicly recognizing the contribution of a child. Paraphrasing is even more powerful in this regard than praise. Paraphrasing encourages further, deeper thinking. Praise often shuts down thinking.

We would invite you to experiment with paraphrasing your students in class and observe the effect it has.

Probing is when the teacher asks a student a follow-up question. Gentle probing (not interrogation) also honors and dignifies student thinking. However, any question sets up a psychological distance between the person asking the question and the person receiving it. For this reason, we like to precede the probe with a paraphrase. The paraphrase serves to grant us tacit permission to ask the follow-up question.

An alternative is to actually teach students the skill of paraphrasing.

CRITERIA FOR DISCERNMENT: HOW DO WE EMBED TRUST IN OUR WORK WITH CHILDREN?

Directions: As you read the following scenarios, identify the four criteria for discernment in terms of the classroom's trustworthiness: teacher competence, teacher respectfulness, teacher personal regard for students, and teacher integrity.

Scenario One: "Skiing Our Way Through Math"

Mr. Roderick has developed a unique approach to the teaching of Grade 8 math. He has identified three levels of readiness, which he has labeled with respect to their degree of challenge using the color coding associated with ski runs (green = foundational, blue = more challenging, and black = most challenging).

Before teaching a unit of study, Mr. Roderick gives the students a diagnostic preassessment. Based on their performance on the preassessment, the student self-selects which level of challenge is most appropriate for him or her for that unit. The green level of challenge is foundational in that it meets all the math benchmarks for student learning for Grade 8. The blue level of challenge is more complex and intellectually rigorous. The black level is very demanding and is often equivalent to work that you might find in the advanced math courses in the high school. The black level is appropriate for only the most able mathematicians. While the basic content of the unit of study remains the same for all three levels, the degrees of challenge are remarkably different.

Initially, Mr. Roderick wondered if most of the students would choose the green level of challenge as it was the easiest. "By Grade 8 a lot of students have developed a fear of math," he said. "And I could understand why some of them might want to select the green level." However, he has faith that the students want to learn and will challenge themselves appropriately, and indeed, the vast majority of the students have consistently selected the blue level. About a quarter of the students chose the green level and about 10 percent selected black. Mr. Roderick allows students to change levels midway through the unit if they discover that the work is either too easy or too difficult. Mr. Roderick stresses continually that there is no stigma attached to the green level. "If the students succeed at the green level, they have achieved every math benchmark for Grade 8. They can be truly proud of themselves."

At the start of the unit, Mr. Roderick prepares an assessment rubric, which he distributes to the students before they select their level of challenge. He likes to use performance assessments that are linked to real-world activities. The most recent one had student groups planning a field trip to India. The green group had to use basic algebra to create and manage a budget for the expenses of the trip. The blue group had several more variables added, together with an unknown to solve for. The black group was planning the same trip to India, but there were multiple unknowns for which the students needed to solve.

Discussion questions

1. What evidence of the criteria for discernment do you see in Mr. Roderick's classroom?

2. How is he attempting to build a supportive and trusting class climate?

3. What elements of emotionally intelligent behavior do you see in the scenario?

Scenario Two: "Are You Changing Your Plan?"

Mrs. Fry greets her first graders at the door of the classroom each morning. The children know and understand the routine. There are two planning boards clearly labeled "Teacher Choice" and "Student Choice." These planning boards reflect Mrs. Fry's approach to the use of learning centers when she works with her students in language arts. Mrs. Fry provides each student with at least two days each week of student choice and at least two days of teacher choice.

On the days when Alice is assigned to teacher choice, Mrs. Fry identifies the learning centers and resources that will match her level of language readiness. On student-choice days, Alice can choose from the eight "pockets" on the student-choice board. These choices offer a wide variety of language-rich activities that tap into student interests and learning styles. For example, on a student-choice day, Alice can select whether she will engage in computer work, a writing task, a drawing activity, or model making. All of these activities are designed to encourage students to use language in entertaining and fun ways. Mrs. Fry has included a system of color coding on the student-choice board. For example, if she recognizes that Alice needs work in written expression, she can tell Alice that she can choose from any of the yellow or red choices, but not from the green or blue.

Mrs. Fry often alternates work at the learning centers so that some children work at the centers while others are free to work directly with her in supervised reading activities or individual conferences.

When a specific student is off task, Mrs. Fry asks if the student is changing his or her plan. The students have come to understand what the question means and quickly return to what they have selected or explain the reasons that their plan has changed.

Discussion Questions

1. What evidence of the criteria for discernment do you see in Mrs. Fry's classroom?

2. How is she attempting to build a supportive and trusting class climate?

3. What elements of emotionally intelligent behavior do you see in the scenario?

CASE STUDY

Directions: Please read the case study below and address the discussion questions.

"Ready for the Teachable Moment!"

As the new teacher on the sixth-grade team, Malcolm Rigby remained quiet and watched the interaction between the veteran members of the team.

"Shall we start out with some general comments on how the unit went?" Michelle Gallsworthy called the meeting together with an invitation. She was in her second year as team leader and wanted to bring greater collaboration to the group. Last year had been fractious, and she was determined to avoid a replay. Having Malcolm on board might help, she thought.

"I thought it went fairly well," Judy Ramikan announced. "I especially liked how Malcolm had the entire sixth grade simulate the circulatory system using colored ribbon and paper plates. Now that's what I call teacher creativity. It was too bad neither of you two were present to see it. You did get his invitation, didn't you?"

"Yes," Michelle responded. "I was sorry to have missed the simulation. I'm sure some excellent learning went on. Are there other comments?"

"I thought the textbook chapter on respiration was too difficult for most of my kids," Rupert Scott announced. "They couldn't answer the questions at the end of the chapter. I had some miserable quiz scores."

"You used the questions at the end of the chapter as a quiz?" Judy asked. Her question managed to combine seeming surprise with "what-on-earth-did-you-expect?" dismissal. "Personally, I don't use textbooks. I find they inhibit teacher creativity. I don't like lockstep lesson planning. One needs to be open and ready for the teachable moment."

"But we have to assess if students actually learned the material," Rupert countered. There was now an edge to his voice. "The textbook allows me to be sure I've covered all the material."

"Coverage versus understanding. We don't seem to have made much progress in the age-old debate," Judy commented.

"Rupert's right. Assessment is important, but it mustn't be too rigid. That kills creativity," Bill Trout interjected.

"Of course it is, but we're not limited to just pencil-and-paper tasks." Judy was gathering a full head of steam. "Haven't you heard about authentic assessment and real-life performance tasks?"

The rhetorical question hung in the air like the memory of last year's discord.

"Shall we review our specific learning objectives?" Michelle attempted to refocus her team. "What knowledge did we want our students to understand, and what skills did we want them to acquire?"

"Critical and creative thinking was high on my list," Judy announced.

"Can we call critical and creative thinking specific learning objectives?" Michelle asked. There was silence for a moment.

"I wanted to differentiate for kids with different learning styles," Rupert murmured.

"An important goal, but is it a specific learning objective?" Michelle turned to Malcolm. "What were some of the learning objectives that you had, Malcolm?"

"I wanted kids to understand something about the various systems that are at work in the human body," Malcolm responded. "And I guess I wanted them to appreciate how complex an organism we really are."

"Wonderment," Judy cut in. "You wanted to nurture wonderment!"

"I wanted to introduce the structure of the written lab report," Rupert added.

"Hands-on activities are what motivate kids," Judy muttered.

"But activities aren't objectives," Malcolm suggested gently. "To be honest, I didn't do very much with the structure of the lab report. I ran out of time."

"Maybe we're trying to achieve too many objectives," Michelle suggested.

"Perhaps we weren't clear enough," Rupert murmured.

"I've said it before and I'll say it again, I don't like the rigidity of the lab report structure," Bill muttered. "I think children need the freedom to organize knowledge in a way that is personally meaningful to them."

"I agree," Malcolm responded. "But is the organization of a lab report the kind of knowledge that we would want students to acquire through discovery learning?"

Silence fell on the science lab. Michelle repressed a smile.

Discussion Questions

1. What different educational belief systems may be present in the case study?

2. What emotionally *unintelligent* behavior do we see in this case study? What might be prompting it? How have the other characters attempted to deal with it? How might you have handled it differently?

8 Bringing It All Together

Teachers as Emotion Coaches

W e ended the last chapter by asking the unaskable question: "What does a teacher do with an unlikable child?" Let's turn the question on its head: "How important is it for a child to like the teacher?"

HOW IMPORTANT IS IT FOR A CHILD TO LIKE THE TEACHER?

The answer would seem to depend on who is doing the answering. We suspect the likeableness of the teacher would be very important to the child and probably to the parents.

For the most part, teachers only hear this question at employment interviews, and in our experience, the responses tend to vary based on whether we are talking with elementary or secondary teachers. Elementary teachers tend to ignore the word *like* and reframe with something along the lines that "creating a warm class climate" is very important. Secondary teachers also tend to avoid responding to the word *like* as though to address it might turn their role in the classroom into some sort of popularity contest. Secondary teachers frequently respond along the following lines: "It's not important whether students like me or not; what's important is that the teacher is respected."

These responses avoid the question, "Is it important for students to like their teachers?" We would respond with a qualified affirmative. If all things are equal, it should be self-evident that children will learn more and more efficiently when they like their teacher as opposed to when they dislike their teacher. In fact, when a child dislikes the teacher (often a reaction to perceiving that the teacher dislikes them), learning is seriously impaired. But please note, our response was a *qualified* affirmative. We will look at possible exceptions later in this chapter.

Short of turning the classroom into a popularity contest, what can a teacher do to make it easier for students to like them? Certainly, skillful communication needs to feature prominently. Teachers who are liked by their students send clear messages and deal with difficult issues in a straightforward manner. They are effective in give-and-take and register emotional cues in attuning their messages. They listen well, seek mutual understanding, and foster open communication.

Teachers who are liked by their students genuinely enjoy the company of children and young adults. Elaine Stinson describes this passion for building relationships in her essay "Teaching Outside the Lines" (as cited in Nieto, 2005):

> I love the relationships I build with my students and their fami-
> lies. This is one of the jewels of teaching and what I have learned
> is that it is the most effective way to inspire learning. It is by
> building deep relationships with my children that I come to
> understand who they are, what they are interested in, what they
> know and are passionate about, what they are curious about, and
> their individual ways of learning. It seems natural to me that chil-
> dren learn best when they are appreciated as whole and unique
> individuals. (p. 107)

Teachers who are liked by their students are the leaders in the classroom, although at times their leadership may be indirect and even delegated to the students. These teachers inspire and guide the performance of others while at the same time holding them accountable for meaningful results. They articulate and arouse enthusiasm for the subject matter and for learning. They lead by example.

Teachers who are liked by their students balance a focus on task accomplishment with attention to maintaining relationships. They promote a highly purposeful, yet friendly and cooperative, class climate. They share learning outcomes, information, and resources and seek out opportunities for collaboration. They create group synergy, draw all students into active and enthusiastic participation, and build team identity, esprit de corps, and commitment.

With all these positive attributes of "likeable" teachers, why would our response to the question be qualified?

Because there are outliers. There are quirky, idiosyncratic, and sometimes temperamental teachers who can be highly effective in the classroom who may not match the description above. These teachers march to the beat of a different drummer. Let's enter the world of Miss Elizabeth Crawley.

THE WORLD ACCORDING TO ELIZABETH CRAWLEY

Elizabeth Crawley wasn't everyone's cup of tea. An aging British spinster, Miss Crawley had taught history since, in her words, "Harold took it in the eye"—reference to the death of King Harold at the Battle of Hastings in 1066. Her hallmarks were an encyclopedic knowledge of history, a caustic and extremely dry sense of humor (Bill once asked her about her goals for the following academic year, and she accused him of planning her funeral), a bouffant hairdo, decidedly Fabian socialist tendencies, sensible shoes, a passion for community service (she volunteered weekly at a local orphanage), and a string of noxious-smelling stray dogs that followed her everywhere including the classroom—thus provoking some very justifiable student and parent complaints (which Elizabeth studiously ignored).

On one occasion, an extremely angry local resident appeared in Miss Crawley's classroom while she was teaching and accused her dogs (which were scattered about the room) of killing his chickens. Without batting an eyelid, Miss Crawley turned away from the furious man and asked her students, with rhetorical flare, "Is it not in the nature of dogs to kill chickens?"

On another occasion, Elizabeth Crawley was asked to substitute for a colleague who was ill. The subject was health, and the ninth graders were midway through a unit on sex education. In response to a student question, Miss Crawley's detailed and graphic explanation was such that it resulted in a number of students, including some fairly boisterous and macho boys, becoming physically ill!

Miss Crawley was a character. She was independent minded, unpredictable, and unconventional. Was she liked by her students? Probably she was liked by a few. But most were in awe of her, fascinated by her eccentricities and, at the same time, a little intimidated by her forthrightness and her odd sense of humor.

But did students learn in Miss Crawley's class? Undoubtedly so; although for the most part, her students only recognized how much they had learned when the course was over. It was fairly common to hear Miss Crawley's ex-students talk about how they had hated her class, but how much they had gotten out of it. There was (and probably still is) a fairly steady flow of appreciative letters to Miss Crawley from past graduates.

So given Miss Crawley's fairly bizarre personality, what was it that made her classroom such a rich learning experience?

Our hunch is that the students saw through her surface eccentricities to her deeply held values. Elizabeth Crawley cared deeply for her students, and they seemed to sense that. Her students recognized that her bluster masked deep compassion—for young adults and, of course, dogs. We suspect that her students also came to understand that Elizabeth had reached a point in her life in which she was socially mature and not dependent on others for evaluation or self-esteem. She was self-directed and self-motivated. She had reached a stage in her adult development in which she was the author of her identity.

And this allows us to use Elizabeth as a segue in order to look at the connections between teacher emotional intelligence and the stages of adult development.

EMOTIONAL INTELLIGENCE: STAGES OF ADULT DEVELOPMENT

In 1982, Robert Kegan wrote a book titled *The Evolving Self* in which he presented a theory of how people become progressively more socially mature as they move through their lives. For the purpose of this chapter, we will use the terms *emotional intelligence* and *social maturity* interchangeably. Kegan defines social maturity as an appreciation of the social world, of emotions and how to manage them. He suggests that there are successive layers of social maturity that people experience as they develop.

Kegan (1982) asserts that the more simple understandings of the social world (as experienced by children and some adolescents) are fundamentally inaccurate. These understandings represent a single and often very egocentric perception. Individuals with this highly subjective perception of the social world are unable to understand what it might be like to see themselves from a perspective other than their own.

For Kegan, being able to appreciate the social world from many different perspectives is the essence of what it means to be objective.

As people develop more and more social perspectives, new layers or stages of social maturity emerge. The layers do not supplant each other, but rather the old becomes embedded in the emerging. Our friend and colleague, Toni Prickett (personal communication, 2009), suggests that fractal development may serve as an appropriate model for Kegan's layers of social maturity in that the previous pattern is repeated to create a new and more complex version. As we develop, our social awareness becomes greater—we become more empathetic and we develop greater flexibility of thought—and so, slowly, we begin the process of emerging from the cocoon of self.

In his later work, *In Over Our Heads: The Mental Demands of Modern Life*, Kegan (1994) suggests that the mental demands of the modern world are developmentally beyond the abilities of many adults. His theory is both constructivist and developmental. He believes that humans make meaning from their environment and create their own understanding from their experiences. This development does not stop when we emerge from adolescence. Adults continue to grow and change over time based upon their life experiences.

Unless we become "stuck" at a particular stage, this process of becoming progressively less subjective repeats itself numerous times during a lifetime. However, Kegan (1994) cautions that few people ever become more socially mature than the majority of their peers.

In this later work, Kegan (1994) suggests that more than half of the adult population are not socially mature enough to meet the demands placed upon them by modern societal institutions such as marriage, the workplace, or school. He suggests that many students, teachers, employees, and marriage partners may expect more understanding from their respective counterparts (teachers from students, spouses from each other, employees from employers and vice versa) than is reasonable to expect. This leads to poor communication, misunderstanding, conflict, and suffering.

While social immaturity in adults is certainly not a good thing (psychologists refer to some such people as narcissists and sociopaths), being socially precocious can be downright dangerous!

In an interview with the magazine *EnlightenNext*, Kegan (Debold & Kegan, 2002) is quoted as saying:

> You have to think about what it means to actually be more complex than what your culture is currently demanding. . . . It's usually a very risky state to be in. I mean, we loved Jesus, Socrates, and Gandhi—after we murdered them. While they were alive, they were a tremendous pain in the ass. Jesus, Abraham Lincoln, Martin Luther King Jr.—These people died relatively young. You don't often live a long life being too far out ahead of your culture. (p. 3)

Essentially, Kegan (1994) proposes three stages (or "orders of consciousness") of adult development that he labels *socializing, self-authoring,* and *self-transformational.* These stages are the ways in which adults make personal meaning in our lives and how we come to define ourselves. Each stage represents a change in how we make meaning of our world and is more complex than the previous one. According to Kegan, we do not leave one stage and enter another. We don't give up previous learning, we transform it.

The implications of Kegan's (1982) stages of adult development for teacher emotional intelligence are interesting. The socializing stage is by far the largest and includes most older adolescents and adults. While the socializing stage represents fairly traditional thinking, the individual has the capacity to think abstractly and can internalize the feelings of others. The socializing individual is also able to respond to the needs of others. However, the socializing individual is driven by the opinions and perceptions of others. Her or his wants are defined by other people's expectations. The socializing individual may actually feel responsible for other people's feelings. The socializing stage of social maturity is ideal for a tribal village where loyalty and stability are of paramount importance.

The socializing teacher finds motivation in the approval and acceptance of others. These others might be students, colleagues, and supervisors. If for example, the socializing teacher is concerned about the approval of students, the focus may be on designing highly engaging and entertaining activities that may lack meaningful coherence or robust learning outcomes. If teachers are striving for the approval of their supervisors, they may find themselves narrowly focused on improving standardized test scores. However, socializing teachers can often work extremely well in collaborative cultures that value teamwork.

The teacher who is at the socializing stage of development finds it fairly easy to take on the perceptions of colleagues and see the world through their eyes. When the school culture is positive, this can result in enhanced collaboration and collegiality. However, when there is a negative culture, the socializing teacher can be readily sucked into it.

Socializing teachers are quite conventional and traditional in their approach to classroom instruction, and while they want and need external validation (praise from colleagues or the principal), they often do not want to be so much in the limelight that they stand out from other teachers. Teachers at this stage of social development understand very well the social needs of elementary school children and are generally well equipped to meet those needs. They will model empathy and explicitly teach sharing and turn taking. However, in the secondary school, the socializing teacher may be perceived as overly conventional and perhaps even boring.

The socializing teacher may be reluctant to accept positions of responsibility that require making potentially difficult or unpopular decisions. We see this commonly when team leaders or heads of department adamantly refuse to have anything to do with the professional evaluation of colleagues.

The next stage of adult development is self-authoring, and Kegan (1982) suggests that less than 50 percent of adults transition into this stage. Self-authoring individuals are modernists and are well suited to a mobile world focused on ideas, science, and the pursuit of truth. Self-authoring individuals have developed their own deeply held values and internal set of rules. Self-authoring individuals are not dependent on others for evaluation or esteem. They are more field independent in the sense that they are self-guided, self-evaluative, and self-motivated. They can be highly efficacious and tend to gravitate in schools toward positions of responsibility. They are not shy about embracing new ideas and may spearhead new initiatives. At best, they can be enormously positive and resourceful. At worst, they can be the bulls in the proverbial china shop.

The self-authoring teacher has internalized a series of values and beliefs about teaching and learning, and professional behavior is guided by those personal values and beliefs. This teacher strives to sculpt an individualized image. Although somewhat of a nonconformist, this educator values independence and autonomy. Prescribed curriculum may be bemoaned as inhibiting teacher creativity, and what are perceived to be "educational fads" may produce skepticism. The self-authoring teacher is self-directed and self-evaluating and may actually find external direction and evaluation demotivating. It is interesting to note that we tend to perceive others through the lens of our own developmental stage. For example, a socializing teacher may perceive a self-authoring principal as overly task oriented, selfish, arrogant, and lacking in appreciation and understanding for staff. On the other hand, a principal who operates at a less developed stage than many of the teachers may be perceived as overly concerned about popular opinion, lacking leadership or courage. In our experience, school leaders who provide support that matches the stage of the teachers' development are more effective in school improvement.

The final stage of social maturity Kegan (1982) refers to as self-transforming. He suggests that very few adults achieve this postmodern stage, and if they do it is usually after the age of forty. Kegan sees this stage as ideal for a world that embraces complexity, chaos, and interactive and adaptive systems. In some regard, Kegan's self-transforming stage shares similarities with Maslow's stage of self-actualization and Erikson's ego-integration. Self-transforming individuals are able to see beyond the limits of their own internal systems. They understand that perceptions are selected and constructed and are open to multiple and even contradictory interpretations. These are the individuals who are constantly inviting us to see things in a different way. They are able to tolerate and even appreciate ambiguity and uncertainty. And they delight in exposing false dichotomies. They tend to see gray as opposed to black and white. They are open to reconsidering and reconstructing what seems at first clear and straightforward. They move from the known toward the unknown, and their lives are rich in small and large ironies.

The self-transformational teacher is able to integrate autonomy and independence with a sense of purpose that is larger than self. In other words, individualism is not perceived as the opposite of collectivism but rather as complementary. Self-transformational teachers are the captains of their destinies and, at the same time, contributing members of a community.

A self-transformational teacher understands that perceptions are personal interpretations of reality that are heavily influenced by assumptions. The self-transformational teacher examines those assumptions and their implications and is open to reconstructing perceptions and literally redefining professional identity.

BRINGING IT ALL TOGETHER: EQ, IDENTITY, AND COACHING

The research cited so far in this book is a testament to the strong connection between teacher emotional intelligence and student learning. The greater the teacher's EQ, the more likely it is that the teacher will be effective in the classroom. There is also a strong connection between the development of our emotional intelligence and our understanding of who we are—our evolving identity. In many ways, our state of social maturity defines how we make sense of the world, how we interact with others, how we construct our perceptions, and how we frame and mold the forces that motivate us. We suggest that as teachers develop more and more complex emotional intelligence and social maturity, they will come to perceive the critical importance of nurturing such emotional growth in others, particularly their students.

So now we are moving from the realm of personal, individual teacher development into the arena of supporting the emotional development of children and young adults.

"But," you may ask, "after all the existential psychology has been put to bed, what does this mean for me on Monday morning when I'm facing 27 sixth graders in Room 407?"

Emotionally intelligent teachers serve as "emotion coaches" for their students.

TEACHERS AS EMOTION COACHES

The term *emotion coach* comes to us from the work of John Gottman (1997). In his laboratory at the University of Washington, Gottman and his research team have studied emotions and emotional awareness in children and adults for many years. While his book *Raising an Emotionally Intelligent Child* (1997) is written for parents, teachers can take an enormous amount from it. Gottman counsels those adults who are most intimately involved with the upbringing of children (parents, teachers, and other caregivers) to be emotion coaches. "Emotion coaches . . . teach their children strategies to deal with life's ups and downs. They don't object to their children's displays of anger, sadness, or fear. Nor do they ignore them. Instead, they accept negative emotions as a fact of life and they use emotional moments as opportunities for teaching . . . important life lessons and building closer relationships" (p. 21).

We all have powerful emotions, and at times these emotions—anger, jealousy, sadness, contempt, scorn, and fear—can be very upsetting. Having the emotions and acting upon them are two different things. Emotionally intelligent teachers understand and employ two of Haim Ginott's (1965) basic principles: (1) All emotions and feelings are permissible, but not all behavior is; and (2) the classroom is not a democracy, and it is the teacher who determines what behavior is permissible.

Teachers can react to student emotions in a number of ways. We think of these responses as the Five Ds. We can respond to student emotions by *dismissing, disapproving, denigrating,* or *dignifying* and *developing.* The latter two (dignify and develop) are the work of the emotion coach.

However, it is often useful in coming to understand a concept to look at what it is not. So let's spend a moment looking at the first three responses to student emotions: dismissal, disapproval, and denigration.

The dismissive teacher doesn't take children's emotions seriously. Many times, adults forget their own childhood and trivialize a child's emotional experience. This is a failure of empathy. In the case of a child feeling strong anxiety about a forthcoming performance in the school play, the well-meaning but misguided teacher might say, "Look, there is absolutely nothing to be frightened of. I've seen you in front of the class; you'll do a great job." Making light of the child's misgivings sends the message that the child's fears are unrealistic, unnecessary, and unworthy of attention. It does not diminish them, nor does it help the child to manage them. It simply serves to drive them underground.

Student sadness is also often dismissed by teachers. We may perceive the traumas of childhood as petty. From the vantage point of adulthood, the broken toy or the momentarily fractured friendship may appear to be a tempest in a teapot, but that will certainly not be the perception of the weeping child. When we consider the source of the upset to be trivial, our reactions can be dismissive. For example, Sally came back to her middle school classroom after the Christmas holidays and appeared dejected and depressed. During the holidays, her pet guinea pig had died. In an attempt to cheer her up, the teacher asked, "Where's that precious smile of yours? Come on, give us a smile! You need to cheer up. It's not like you've lost your best friend!" However well intentioned the teacher may have been, Sally received the message that her feelings were unacceptable and her grief was somehow foolish.

IRSHAD AND MELVIN: SEPARATING EMOTIONS FROM BEHAVIOR

Teachers can also show that they disapprove of some emotions. Perhaps the most commonly disapproved of emotion in children is anger. Imagine the following situation: Melvin and Irshad are playing with blocks in the "construction corner" of the kindergarten classroom. Up until now, both boys have engaged primarily in parallel play. Suddenly, Irshad announces he is building an airport and needs the dump truck. Before Irshad can pick up the toy dump truck, Melvin has seized it and has "driven" it into his "building site." A quarrel erupts. Irshad snatches the truck from Melvin, calls him a "stealer," and throws a block at him.

In this case, the teacher took Irshad to task for his display of anger. She told him in no uncertain terms that such anger was unacceptable in the classroom, and she had him sit on the time-out chair for twenty minutes. The teacher scolded and punished the emotion. She sent the clear message that Irshad's anger was unacceptable. This is a very different message than to say that his behavior was unacceptable. Irshad had a right to his anger. He had announced a claim on the toy truck, only to find that his classmate had summarily commandeered it.

In a similar situation, most adults would find themselves at least irritated if not furious. Imagine being in a crowded parking lot, finally finding the one unoccupied space, and putting on your signal light to indicate your intention to claim the space only to have another driver push ahead of you and claim the space. Only the most docile among us would fail to bare their canines!

Irshad may have had a right to his anger, but he certainly didn't have a right to his unacceptable behavior—the name-calling and throwing of the block. We believe the teacher would have been more effective in dealing with Irshad if she had empathized with his frustration but firmly declared his behavior unacceptable. When we confuse emotions and behavior, we inhibit the growth of emotional intelligence. It is only when teachers and students recognize and accept their emotions that they can begin the process of managing them constructively.

Teachers who denigrate student emotions often do so without intending to cause harm. These are adults who laugh at the righteous indignation of a toddler or tease a shy middle school student for being fearful and anxious. These teachers may think that their laughter will reduce the child's anger or that teasing will "toughen" the child up—help them to get over their insecurities. The opposite is more likely to be the case.

Emotionally intelligent teachers actively dignify and develop their students' EQ. They foster supportive learning communities in their classroom by serving as emotional field guides to their students. They recognize and dignify even negative emotions, set limits on inappropriate behavior, and teach students how to manage their strong feelings, discover constructive outlets, and resolve problems.

The following five steps of emotion coaching are adapted from Gottman's (1997) work.

1. Become aware of the child's or student's emotion

2. Recognize the emotional moment as an opportunity for relationship building and teaching

3. Listen empathetically in order to validate the student's feelings

4. Support the child or student in finding the words to label the emotion that he or she is having

5. Set behavioral limits while exploring strategies to solve the problem at hand

It is clear from the above steps that the teacher who serves as an emotion coach has to have a considerable degree of emotional intelligence.

First, the teacher needs to be able to recognize emotions in children and young people. Interestingly, we are not all equally sensitive to the different emotions. For example, some of us may have a much greater sensitivity to anger in others, while others may be more aware of anxiety or fear. Gottman (1997) has produced a series of emotional-awareness self-tests that allow teachers and parents greater insight into how and why we react as we do to other people's emotions. Most important, Gottman's research clearly suggests that such emotional awareness can be developed over time.

Second, the teacher who engages in emotion coaching needs be able to perceive emotional situations as opportunities. Too many of us perceive such emotional moments with discomfort, anxiety, or outright fear. It may be that emotions such as anger conjure within us as sense of losing control or "flying off the handle" and we default to avoidance behaviors. This can lead to dismissing or disapproving of such emotions in our students.

Third, the emotion coach listens empathetically in order to validate the student's feelings. This can be accomplished by paraphrasing both the emotion and the content—most often with the emotion first. For example, we might say to Irshad, "You're very angry because Melvin took the truck you wanted to play with." Our work in Cognitive Coaching suggests that it is often impossible to support someone in problem-resolving efforts before the coach has "honored the existing state"—and the existing troubled state is often characterized by strong feelings of emotion. When we honor the existing state, we dignify the problem and the emotion associated with it. We don't dwell upon the negative, but we do paraphrase the emotion and so validate it.

Fourth, the emotion coach then supports the student in finding appropriate labels for the emotions experienced. The labeling process is psychologically important. When we name something, we gain a degree of distance from it and a degree of control over it. By naming our emotions we begin to become their authors and managers rather than the other way around. Research studies indicate that the act of naming our emotions has a soothing effect on the nervous system, and thus assists children to recover more quickly from an upsetting incident. Gottman's theory (1997) as to how this may work neurologically is that the act of talking about an emotion as you are experiencing it engages the left hemisphere of the brain, which is the center of language and logic. This takes the focus away from the emotion-creating amygdala and assists the child (or adult) in calming down. Over time, it also supports the child in developing self-soothing strategies, which are the foundation of emotional resilience.

The emotionally intelligent teacher also recognizes that intense emotional situations are opportunities for relationship building. Even school tragedies, such as student or teacher deaths, when handled with care and compassion can serve to bring individuals together. Only a few months after his retirement from the position of assistant principal at the International School of Kuala Lumpur, Tim Tarleton suddenly and unexpectedly passed away. Tim had a gentle and wise manner and was much loved and admired by students and colleagues alike. Teachers, students, and administrators came together to plan a memorial service. Collectively, the young and the old expressed their sadness, grief, and fears. Many tears were shed, and many relationships were strengthened.

When adults display emotionally intelligent behavior, for example, handling anger or disappointment constructively, they serve as role models for children and young adults.

Gottman's (1997) research on parents who consistently practice emotion coaching with their children indicates that these children have better physical health and score higher academically than children whose parents do not offer such guidance. The implications for teachers are clear.

To bring it all together, it is clear that the influence of an emotionally intelligent teacher, the teacher who is an emotion coach, does not end when the school year closes in June. Goleman (2006) suggests that there are long-term positive residual effects on students. He cites a study that showed that children who had an emotionally connected teacher in first grade were still earning better grades in the sixth grade. "Good teachers are like good parents. By offering a secure base, a teacher creates an environment that lets students' brains function at their best" (p. 283).

Our commitment to students, their learning, the school we work for, the colleagues we work with, indeed our commitment to the teaching profession, grows out of emotional bonding. The passion and pride that we take in the craft of teaching are forged in the furnace of our relationships and become the very mettle of our professional identities as emotionally intelligent teachers.

References

Amabile, T. M., Barsade, S. G., Mueller, J. S., & Staw, B. M. (2005). Affect and creativity at work. *Administrative Science Quarterly, 50,* 367–403.

Aristotle. (2006). *Nicomachean ethics* (W. D. Ross, Trans.). Retrieved from http:// ebooks.adelaide.edu.au/a/aristotle/nicomachean

Aronson, E. (2008). *The social animal* (10th ed.). New York: Worth.

An atheist in the woods. (2007, February). Retrieved from www.ourlighterside .com/stuff/atheistinwoods

Ayan, S. (2009, April). How humor makes you friendlier, sexier. *Scientific American Mind, 20*(2). Retrieved from www.scientificamerican.com/article.cfm?id=laughing-matters

Ballantyne, R. M. (1857). *The coral island.* Edinburgh, UK: W. & R. Chambers.

Bar-On, R., & Parker, D. A. (2000). *Handbook of emotional intelligence: Theory, development, assessment and application at home, school, and in the workplace.* San Francisco: Jossey-Bass.

Barsade, S., & Gibson, D. (2007, February). Why does affect matter in organizations? *Academy of Management Perspectives,* 36–59.

Barth, R. (1990). *Improving schools from within: Teachers, parents and principals can make a difference.* San Francisco: Jossey-Bass.

BBC World Service News. (2009, May 23). China bridge jumper "gets a push." *BBC News.* Retrieved from http://news.bbc.co.uk/2/hi/asia-pacific/8064867.stm

Brooks, R., & Goldstein, S. (2001). *Raising resilient children.* New York: McGraw-Hill.

Brophy, J. (1983). Research on the self-fulfilling prophecy and teacher expectations. *Journal of Educational Psychology, 75,* 631–661.

Brown, R., & Kulik, J. (1977). Flashbulb memories. *Cognition, 5,* 73–99.

Bruner, J. (1996). *The culture of education.* Cambridge, MA: Harvard University Press.

Bryk, A., & Schneider, B. (2004). *Trust in schools: A core resource for development.* New York: Russell Sage.

Caine, R. N., & Caine, G. (1994). *Making connections: Teaching and the human brain.* Reading, MA: Addison-Wesley.

Campbell, L., & Campbell, B. (1999). *Multiple intelligences and student achievement success stories from six schools.* Alexandria, VA: Association for Supervision and Curriculum Development.

Campos, J., & Sternberg, C. (1981). Perception, appraisal, and emotion: The onset of social referencing. In M. Lamb & L. Sherrod (Eds.), *Infant social cognition: Empirical and theoretical considerations* (pp. 273–314). Hillsdale, NJ: Lawrence Erlbaum.

Churchill, W. (1952, November 4). Prime minister address to the British House of Commons in Westminster, England. Retrieved from www.winston churchill.org/component/content/article/16-quotes/484-house-of-commons-4-november-1952-

Cohen, E. G., & Lotan, R. A. (1997). *Working for equity in heterogeneous classrooms: Sociological theory in practice.* New York: Teachers College Press.

Cooper, H. M., & Tom, D. Y. H. (1984). Teacher expectation research: A review with implications for classroom instruction. *Elementary School Journal, 85,* 76–89.

Costa, A., & Garmston, R. (2002). *Cognitive coaching: A foundation for Renaissance schools.* Norwood, MA: Christopher-Gordon.

Costa, A., & Garmston, R. (2007). *Cognitive coaching foundation seminar learning guide* (7th ed.). Highlands Ranch, CO: Center for Cognitive Coaching.

Covey, S. (2004). *7 habits of highly effective people.* New York: Free Press.

Crabtree, S. (2004, June 4). Teachers who care get the most from kids. *Detroit News,* p. 9.

Csikszentmihalyi, M. (1991). *Flow: The psychology of optimal experience.* New York: Harper Perennial.

Cushman, K. (2003). *Fires in the bathroom: Advice for teachers from high school students.* New York: The New Press.

Dalai Lama & Ekman, P. (2008). *Emotional awareness: Overcoming the obstacles to psychological balance and compassion.* New York: Henry Holt.

Damasio, A. (1994). *Descartes' error: Emotion, reason, and the human brain.* New York: Penguin.

Darwin, C. (1872). *The expression of the emotions in man and animals.* London: Murray.

Davis, M. H., & Kraus, L. A. (1997). Personality and empathic accuracy. In W. Ickes (Ed.), *Empathic accuracy* (pp. 144–168). New York: Guilford Press.

Debold, E. (Interviewer), & Kegan, R. (Interviewee). (2002, Fall/Winter). Epistemology, fourth order consciousness, and the subject-object relationship or . . . how the self evolves: An interview with Robert Kegan. *EnlightenNext Magazine.* Retrieved from www.enlightennext.org/magazine/j22/kegan.asp

de Gelder, B., Vroomen, J., Pourtois, G., & Weiskrantz, L. (1999). Non-conscious recognition of affect in the absence of striate cortex. *NeuroReport, 10,* 3759–3763.

Denzin, N. K. (1984). *On understanding emotion.* San Francisco: Jossey-Bass.

de Waal, F. (n.d.). *Frans de Waal: Quotes.* Retrieved July 13, 2009, from www .absoluteastronomy.com/topics/Frans_de_Waal

Dewey, J. (2001). *The school and society: The child and the curriculum.* Mineola, NY: Dover.

Dickens, C. (2007). *Hard times.* New York: Simon & Schuster. (Original work published 1854)

Dilts, R. (1994). *Effective presentation skills.* Capitola, CA: Meta.

Eisenberger, N. I., & Lieberman, M. D. (2004). Why rejection hurts: A common neural alarm system for physical and social pain. *Trends in Cognitive Sciences, 8,* 294–300.

Ekman, P. (2003). *Emotions revealed: Recognizing faces and feelings to improve communication and emotional life.* New York: Henry Holt.

Ekman, P. (n.d.). METT: Micro expression training tool [Training program]. Retrieved May 3, 2009, from www.paulekman.com

Elfenbein, H. A., Foo, M., White, J., Tan, H., & Aik, V. (2007). Reading your counterpart: The benefit of emotion recognition accuracy for effectiveness in negotiation. *Journal of Nonverbal Behavior, 31,* 205–223.

Emerson, R. W. (n.d.). *World of quotes: Historic quotes and proverbs.* Retrieved from www.worldofquotes.com/author/Ralph-Waldo-Emerson/1/index.html

Freire, P. (1998). *Teachers as cultural workers: Letters to those who dare to teach.* Boulder, CO: Westview.

Freud, S. (1989). *Civilization and its discontents.* New York: W. W. Norton. (Original work published 1930)

Garmston, R. (2005). *The presenter's fieldbook: A practical guide.* Norwood, MA: Christopher-Gordon.

Garmston, R., & Wellman, B. (2009). *The adaptive school: A sourcebook for developing collaborative groups* (2nd ed.). Norwood, MA: Christopher-Gordon.

George, J. M. (1991). State or trait: Effects of positive mood on prosocial behaviors at work. *Journal of Applied Psychology, 76,* 299–307.

Ginott, H. (1965). *Between parent and child.* New York: Macmillan.

Ginott, H. (1995). *Teacher and child: A book for parents and teachers.* New York: Collier.

Gladwell, M. (2005). *Blink: The power of thinking without thinking.* Boston: Little, Brown.

Goldberg, C. (2008, March 6). East and West: Seeing the world through different lenses. *International Herald Tribune,* p. 11.

Goldfried, M. R., & Robins, C. J. (1983). Self-schema, cognitive bias and the processing of therapeutic experiences. In P. C. Kendall (Ed.), *Advances in cognitive-behavioral research and therapy* (Vol. 2, pp. 33–80). San Diego, CA: Academic Press.

Golding, W. (1954). *The lord of the flies.* New York: Perigree Books.

Goldin-Meadow, S. (1997). When gestures and words speak differently. *Current Directions in Psychological Science, 6,* 138–143.

Goldin-Meadow, S., Wagner Cook, S., & Mitchell, Z. A. (2009). Gesturing gives children new ideas about math. *Psychological Science, 20,* 267–272.

Goleman, D. (1995). *Emotional intelligence: Why it can matter more than IQ.* New York: Bantam Books.

Goleman, D. (1998). *Working with emotional intelligence.* New York: Bantam Books.

Goleman, D. (2001). *The emotionally intelligent workplace.* San Francisco: Jossey-Bass.

Goleman, D. (2006). *Social intelligence: The new science of social relationships.* New York: Bantam Books.

Good, T. L. (1987). Two decades of research on teacher expectations: Findings and future directions. *Journal of Teacher Education, 38*(4), 32–47.

Gordon, R., & Cruz, J. (2003). Simulation theory. *Encyclopedia of cognitive science* (Vol. 4, pp. 9–14). London: Macmillan.

Gottman, J. (with Declaire, J.). (1997). *Raising an emotionally intelligent child: The heart of parenting.* New York: Simon & Schuster.

Grandin, T. (1995). *Thinking in pictures: My life with autism.* New York: Vintage Books.

Grinder, M. (1991). *Righting the educational conveyor belt.* Portland, OR: Metamorphous Press.

Guskey, T. (2000). Twenty questions? Twenty tools for better teaching. *Principal Leadership, 1*(3), 5–7.

Hargreaves, A. (2001). Emotional geographies of teaching. *Teachers College Record, 103,* 1056–1080.

Hariri, A. R., Bookheimer, S. Y., & Mazziotta, J. C. (2000). Modulating emotional responses: Effects of a neocortical network on the limbic system. *NeuroReport, 11*, 43–48.

Hatfield, E., Cacioppo, J. T., & Rapson, R. L. (1993). Emotional contagion. *Current Directions in Psychological Science, 2*, 96–99.

Hatfield, E., Cacioppo, J. T., & Rapson, R. L. (1994). *Emotional contagion.* New York: Cambridge University Press.

Haviland, J. J., & Malatesta, C. Z. (1981). The development of sex differences in nonverbal signals: Fallacies, facts, and fantasies. In C. Mayo & N. M. Henley (Eds.), *Gender and nonverbal behavior* (pp. 183–208). New York: Springer-Verlag.

Heider, F. (1958). *The psychology of interpersonal relationships.* New York: Wiley.

Hellison, D. (2003). *Teaching responsibility through physical activity* (2nd ed.). Champaign, IL: Human Kinetics.

Herzberg, F. I. (1987, September/October). One more time: How do you motivate employees? *Harvard Business Review, 65*(5), 109–120.

House, J. S., Landis, K. R., & Umberson, D. (1988, July 29). Social relationships and health. *Science, 241*, 540–545.

Howes, M. J., Hokanson, J. E., & Lowenstein, D. A. (1985). Induction of depressive affect after prolonged exposure to a mildly depressed individual. *Journal of Personality and Social Psychology, 49*, 1110–1113.

Hu, W. (2009, April 4). Gossip girls and boys get lessons in empathy. *New York Times.* Retrieved from www.nytimes.com/2009/04/05/education/05empathy.html?scp=1&sq=gossip%20girls%20and%20boys&st=cseWeb

Hunter, M., & Barker, G. (1987). "If at first . . .": Attribution theory in the classroom. *Educational Leadership, 45*(2), 50–54.

Iacoboni, M. (2008). *Mirroring people: The new science of how we connect with others.* New York: Farrar, Straus & Giroux.

James, W. (1950). *The principles of psychology* (Vols. 1–2). Mineola, NY: Dover. (Original work published 1890)

Jensen, D. (2004). *Walking on water: Reading, writing and revolution.* White River Junction, VT: Chelsea Green.

Jensen, E. (2005). *Teaching with the brain in mind* (2nd ed.). Alexandria, VA: Association for Supervision and Curriculum Development.

Joyce, B., & Showers, B. (1980). Improving inservice training: The messages of research. *Educational Leadership, 37*, 379–385.

Joyce, B., & Showers, B. (2002). *Student achievement through staff development* (3rd ed.). Alexandria, VA: Association for Supervision and Curriculum Development.

Judge, T. A. (1993). Does affective disposition moderate the relationship between job satisfaction and voluntary turn-over? *Journal of Applied Psychology, 78*, 395–401.

Judge, T. A., Thoresen, C. J., Bono, J. E., & Patton, G. K. (2001). The job satisfaction–job performance relationship: A qualitative and quantitative review. *Psychological Bulletin, 127*, 376–407.

Kegan, R. (1982). *The evolving self: Problem and process in human development.* Cambridge, MA: Harvard University Press.

Kegan, R. (1994). *In over our heads: The mental demands of modern life.* Cambridge, MA: Harvard University Press.

Kelley, H. (1967). Attribution theory in social psychology. In D. Levine (Ed.), *Nebraska symposium on motivation* (pp. 192–238). Lincoln: University of Nebraska Press.

Kohn, A. (1999). *Punished by rewards: The trouble with gold stars, incentive plans, A's, praise, and other bribes*. New York: Houghton Mifflin.

Kuhn, T. S. (1962). *The structure of scientific revolutions* (1st ed.). Chicago: University of Chicago Press.

Kusuma-Powell, O., & Powell, W. (2000, December). The pedagogy of the pressured: Does rigorous mean onerous? *IB World, 28*.

Lachman, R., Lachman, J. L., & Butterfield, E. C. (1979). *Cognitive psychology and information processing*. Hillsdale, NJ: Erlbaum.

LaFrance, M., & Broadbent, M. (1976). Group rapport: Posture sharing as a nonverbal indicator. *Group and Organizational Studies, 1*, 328–333.

Landsman, J., Moore, T., & Simmons, R. (2008, March). Reluctant teachers, reluctant learners. *Educational Leadership, 65*(6), 62–66.

Lang, W. (Director), Brackett, C. (Producer), & Zanuck, D. (Producer). (1956). *The king and I* [Motion picture]. United States: Twentieth Century Fox.

Langer, G., & Colton, A. (2005, February). Looking at student work. *Educational Leadership, 62*(5), 22–26.

LeDoux, J. (1996). *The emotional brain: The mysterious underpinnings of emotional life*. New York: Simon & Schuster.

Lyubomirsky, S., King, L., & Diener, E. (2005). The benefits of frequent positive affect: Does happiness lead to success? *Psychological Bulletin, 131*, 803–855.

MacLean, P. D. (1990). *The triune brain in evolution: Role in paleocerebral functions*. New York: Plenum Press.

Mayer, J., & Salovey, P. (1997). What is emotional intelligence. In P. Salovey & D. Sluyter (Eds.), *Emotional development and emotional intelligence* (pp. 3–31). New York: Basic Books.

Medina, J. (2008). *Brain rules: 12 principles for surviving and thriving at work, home, and school*. Seattle, WA: Pear Press.

Millet, C., Johnson, S., Cooper, C., Donald, I., Cartwright, S., & Taylor, P. (2005, January). *Britain's most stressful occupations and the role of emotional labour*. Presentation at the British Psychological Society, Division of Occupational Psychology Annual Conference, Warwick, UK.

Neill, A. S. (1992). *Summerhill school: A new view of childhood*. New York: St. Martins Press.

Niedenthal, P., Krauth-Gruber, S., & Ric, F. (2006). *Psychology of emotions*. New York: Psychology Press.

Nieto, S., (Ed.). (2005). *Why we teach*. New York: Teachers College Press.

Nietzsche, F. (1916). *Thus spake Zarathustra: A book for all and none* (T. Commons, Trans.). New York: Macmillan.

Nisbett, R. (2003). *The geography of thought: How Asians and Westerners think differently . . . and why*. New York: The Free Press.

No Child Left Behind Act of 2001. 20 U.S.C. § 6301 *et seq.* (2002).

Pert, C. (1997). *Molecules of emotion: The science behind mind-body medicine*. New York: Touchstone.

Plutchik, R. (1994). *The psychology and biology of emotion*. New York: HarperCollins.

Popkewitz, T. (1998). *Struggling for the soul: The politics of schooling and the construction of the teacher*. New York: Teachers College Press.

Powell, W. (1998). On marshmallows, rings, and rats. *International Schools Journal, 17*(2), 41–51.

Powell, W., & Kusuma-Powell, O. (2007a). *Making the difference: Differentiation in international schools.* Washington, DC: U.S. Department of State, Office of Overseas Schools.

Powell, W., & Kusuma-Powell, O. (2007b, October). *Who are we teaching?* Keynote address presented at the Association of International Schools Administrators' Conference, Johannesburg, South Africa.

Ramachandran, V. S. (2000, May 29). Mirror neurons and imitation learning as the driving force behind "the great leap forward" in human evolution. *Edge, 69.* Retrieved from www.edge.org/3rd_culture/ramachandran/ramachandran_p1.html

Ramachandran, V. S., & Blakeslee, S. (1998). *Phantoms in the brain: Probing the mysteries of the human mind.* New York: HarperCollins.

Rogers, C. (1961). *On becoming a person.* Boston: Houghton Mifflin.

Rosenthal, R., & Jacobson, L. (1992). *Pygmalion in the classroom: Teacher expectation and pupils' intellectual development.* New York: Irvington.

Ross, L. (1977). The intuitive psychologist and his shortcomings: Distortions in the attribution process. In L. Berkowitz (Ed.), *Advances in experimental social psychology* (Vol. 10, 173–220). San Diego, CA: Academic Press.

Rousseau, J.-J. (1993). *Emile* (B. Foxley, Trans.). London: Orion. (Original work published 1762)

Rudduck, J., Day, J., & Wallace, G. (1997). Students' perspectives on school improvement. In A. Hargreaves (Ed.), *1997 ASCD year book: Rethinking educational change with heart and mind* (pp. 73–91). Alexandria, VA: Association for Supervision and Curriculum Development.

Sanford, C. (1995). *Myths of organizational effectiveness at work.* Battle Ground, WA: Springhill.

Sapolsky, R. (2004). *Why zebras don't get ulcers* (3rd ed.). New York: Henry Holt.

Selye, H. (1975). Confusion and controversy in the stress field. *Journal of Human Stress, 1*(2), 37–44.

Shakespeare, W. (2004). *Othello* (Folger Shakespeare Library Edition). New York: Simon & Schuster. (Original work published 1623)

Shoda, Y., Mischel, W., & Peake, P. K. (1990). Predicting adolescent cognitive and self-regulatory competencies from preschool delay of gratification: Identifying diagnostic conditions. *Developmental Psychology, 26,* 978–986.

Skinner, B. F. (1971). *Beyond freedom and dignity.* Indianapolis, IN: Hackett.

Snyder, M., Tanke, E. D., & Berscheid, E. (1977). Social perception and interpersonal behavior: On the self-fulfilling nature of social stereotypes. *Journal of Personality and Social Psychology, 35,* 656–666.

Solzhenitsyn, A. (1970). *Solzhenitsyn's 1970 Nobel lecture in literature.* Presented to the Swedish Academy, Stockholm.

Stevens, S. (1997). *Classroom success for the LD and ADHD child.* Winston-Salem, NC: John F. Blair.

Swann, W. B., Jr., & Read, S. J. (1981). Self-verification processes: How we sustain our self-conceptions. *Journal of Experimental Social Psychology, 17,* 351–372.

Sylwester, R. (2007). *The adolescent brain: Reaching for autonomy.* Thousand Oaks, CA: Corwin.

Taylor, S. (2006). Tend and befriend: Biobehavioral bases of affiliation under stress. *Current Directions in Psychological Science, 15,* 273–277.

Thompson, M. (2000, July 5). *Narrative therapy in schools*. Keynote address presented at the Association for International School Heads (AISH) Summer Seminar, Washington, DC.

Truffaut, F. (Director). (1976). *Small change* [Motion picture]. United States: Metro Goldwyn Mayer.

Tyler, R. (1949). *Basic principles of curriculum and instruction*. Chicago: University of Chicago Press.

Van Overwalle, F., & De Metsenaere, M. (1990). The effects of attribution-based intervention and study strategy training on academic achievement in college freshmen. *British Journal of Educational Psychology, 60,* 299–311.

Vygotsky, L. S. (1978). *Mind and society: The development of higher mental processes*. Cambridge, MA: Harvard University Press.

Wade, N. (2006). *Before the dawn: Recovering the lost history of our ancestors*. New York: Penguin.

Wells, H. G. (1920). *The outline of history* (Vol. 2). New York: Doubleday.

Whitehead, A. (n.d.). *Alfred North Whitehead quotes*. Retrieved September 14, 2009, from http://thinkexist.com/quotes/alfred_north_whitehead

Willis, J. (2007). *Brain friendly strategies for the inclusion classroom*. Alexandria, VA: Association for Supervision and Curriculum Development.

Witkin, H. M., Goodenough, D., & Coc, P. (1975). *Field dependent and field independent cognitive styles and their implications*. Princeton, NJ: Educational Testing Service.

Wyss, J. (2007). *The Swiss family Robinson*. New York: Penguin. (Original work published 1813)

Yimou, Z. (Director). (2000). *Not one less* [Motion picture]. United States: Sony Pictures.

Index

CORWIN

A SAGE Company

The Corwin logo—a raven striding across an open book—represents the union of courage and learning. Corwin is committed to improving education for all learners by publishing books and other professional development resources for those serving the field of PreK–12 education. By providing practical, hands-on materials, Corwin continues to carry out the promise of its motto: **"Helping Educators Do Their Work Better."**